ACCLAIM FOR *REACH BEYOND*

"My friend Lou Vickery has done an excellent job with his new book, *Reach Beyond.* Lou has been in life's toughest arenas. He understands. This book is 'must' reading."

—Bill (Bubba) Bussey, Co-host of the Rick & Bubba Radio Show

"*Reach Beyond* is a rich resource of gems blended with stories, illustrations, quotes, and life-changing insights. Its pages will satisfy the hunger for knowing the path to success. With unique wisdom and valuable advice, *Reach Beyond* offers readers the path to turn the ordinary into extraordinary."

—Janet Perez Eckles, International Speaker and Author

"*Reach Beyond* is the quintessential primer for life. It contains the thoughts and beliefs and secrets of a life well lived. It teaches the reader how to live more productively. This is a must-read survival guide. Reading this book can literally help the reader navigate the current times with ease and purpose. I highly recommend this book."

—Dr. Ted Broer, CEO of Healthmasters.com

"*Reach Beyond* is a perfect companion book for your life. Use it as a guide to embracing who you are and where you are going. When used daily, it can help take you to the next level. It is an interactive work with each chapter giving you tons to ponder. It hit a home run with me . . . pun intended! One of Lou's best."

—Elizabeth Chryst, Retired GOP Secretary, US Senate

"Lou Vickery has masterfully woven a self-analysis manual that leaves us optimistic about ourselves and our future. *Reach Beyond* is packed full of common-sense, practical solutions and poignant anecdotes. The reader will gain much from this book."

—Bob Beauprez, Retired US House of Representatives, Colo

Indigo River Publishing
3 West Garden Street, Ste. 718
Pensacola, FL 32502
www.indigoriverpublishing.com

Reach Beyond—And Find Your Path To Success | Lou Vickery, author
ISBN 978-1-950906-63-5 (paperback), 978-1-950906-64-2 (ebook)
LCCN 2020933100

Edited by Tim Neller and Regina Cornell
Cover design by Robin Vuchnich
Interior design by Nikkita Kent

Special discounts are available on quantity purchases by corporations, associations, and others. For details, contact the publisher at the address above.

Orders by US trade bookstores and wholesalers: Please contact the publisher at the address above.

With Indigo River Publishing, you can always expect great books,
strong voices, and meaningful messages.
Most importantly, you'll always find . . . words worth reading.

REACH BEYOND

AND FIND YOUR PATH TO SUCCESS

LOU
VICKERY

CONTENTS

PREFACE

It is great having you here! You cannot imagine how excited I am that you have joined me. Your presence makes me feel really awesome. It also elevates my responsibility immensely. It is now up to me to use the pages in this book to provide significant insight and direction that will help you see a you that you have never seen before.

I may not know you personally. I may not know your history. I may not know where you live or what you do for a living. What I do know is that you are a uniquely talented person ready to reach beyond and grasp something better.

It is my desire that my words will touch your inner being in such a way that it provides you a deeper perspective of yourself. I want you to connect to the infinite possibilities that exist in you right now—where you are and just as you are. I want you to divorce yourself from old, antiquated ways that don't fit you anymore. I want you to align with a new you.

The life lessons found between these two covers are designed to instruct, inform, and inspire you to generate a more thorough thought process about what it takes to survive, strive, then thrive. Hopefully, these messages will help you stretch out and reach beyond the way it is for the greater reward of the way it can be. I can sense we are sharing this time together because you want to assess life in a bigger and broader way. Am I right?

I realize as I say that, a real part of your psyche will want to hold on to a view of yourself that is a small fraction of what you can become. A little inner voice will argue for the safe, the predictable, the comfortable ways of the past. Let me caution you about the tendency to argue for your limitations and being zealously obsessed with why you can't do something.

There will be countless opportunities in this book to question those habitual beliefs that possibly have held you back. You will definitely find substance here that will help you develop the necessary backbone and inner strength to overcome viewpoints that up to now have limited your perception and thwarted your ability to reach beyond to engage new levels of growth and prosperity. I want you to lean heavily on that part of you that is ready to reach beyond in a more creative and expansive way to see the possible instead of the impossible.

An important step in reaching beyond is to expand your awareness. Awareness is what will allow you to come alive to the greatness you have within. When awareness is small, you think small. You think in terms like "just getting by." But when you enlarge your awareness, you explore in greater depth those totally unique gifts that are just waiting for you to awaken.

I don't think there is any question that you will raise your awareness as we delve into an exploration of challenge and high adventure, is there? So come with me now as we work through the changes in your life that your heart is calling you to make. For sure, the price will be great, but the rewards will be even greater.

***

History is *his-story* of the past. Here is a brief summary of my history.

I am in the fourth quarter of life. It has been an incredible journey. Yes, I have regrets. There are things I wish I hadn't done and things I realize I should have done. But there are many things I am really pleased to have done. It all makes up a lifetime, doesn't it?

I have been in every state in the continental United States. I have visited every city over 150,000 in population. I have seen all the great sights in this country, from coast to coast. I have met hundreds of thousands of people. I have rubbed shoulders with highly successful people from all walks of life, from athletes to businessmen to world leaders. I have been blessed by so much great exposure to those who found the secret to moving beyond.

From this great exposure, I have heard some of the most incredible stories from those who have been in life's toughest arenas. I am excited to share their experience and wisdom. These individuals somewhere along the line learned the value of reaching beyond. They created a higher capacity for improvement, expanded their intellectual curiosity, enlarged their creative imagination, and rearranged their lives to grow beyond what they were before.

This book was not designed to be read in one sitting. It has all of the astuteness of a resource book. Use it to supplement your efforts as you face life's greatest challenges and opportunities. But be careful that you don't set the book on a shelf where it will collect dust and be relegated to posterity. Keep it close to your favorite relaxing place. Give yourself—and me—a chance to see how you can step beyond the ordinary into the world of the extraordinary.

There may be only one life message that helps relocate you beyond where you are. Then again, there may be several that do, and some that may even emerge that have been hidden under layers of denial. Whatever may be the case, you will find something here that will help you get from where you are to where you want to be.

I wish for you a bright forever.

To experience something different, you must decide to reach beyond the way it is to enjoy something different because if you keep doing what you have always done, you won't even keep getting the same results you have always gotten. The world of attitudes, skills, methods, and tactics are constantly changing, calling you to reach beyond with a newfound vision the hurdles you face to land on success.

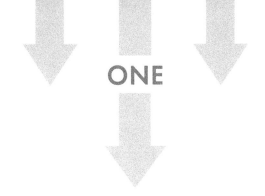

ONE

FOCUS ON THE DASH

Fairy tales often begin with "Once upon a time" and end with "And they lived happily ever after." It is between those two pages where the tale is actually told, isn't it?

How are you doing with your fairy tale? Maybe you haven't thought of it this way, but isn't the most important thing on a gravestone the dash between the date of birth and the date of death? That is where the real-life story—the real fairy tale—is told, don't you think?

The dash is filled with a mixture of successes, struggles, and setbacks. The successes are what keep us going despite the struggles. Unfortunately for some, the price of pushing beyond the struggles is too high a price to pay.

All of us at some point in our lives experience wounds that are unseen. Many of us have faced the potentially paralyzing grip of failure. Life grants no immunities to challenges that sometimes appear beyond our ability to cope. To be human is to fight internal battles deep within ourselves and live with silent pain. It is in these invisible battles where one's story often unfolds and the fairy tale is created. Is that a reasonable assumption?

I mentioned some of my past in the preface. I want to recount some additional history here to assure you that my old writing pen has been dipped in a deep well of varied and broad experiences.

I have had four distinctively different careers. I have been a professional baseball player, a stockbroker, a salesperson and sales trainer, and a radio talk show host.

My personal dash over these years has known the depths of the valleys and the peaks of the mountains. My dash has also experienced a lot of "almosts." I have been at that "almost" place many times in my life. Do you know what I mean?

My life travels have taken me along routes that had many unplanned detours, as well. Some of these detours bordered on ruin.

I have experienced some of life's worst struggles along these detours. From a failed career to a failed business, legal issues, a broken marriage, the death of a nineteen-year-old stepson, and not knowing where my next paycheck would come from, all have given me ample opportunities to experience what it takes to reach beyond.

Many times, I have asked myself, *What else can possibly go wrong? How much more can I handle?* Have these questions ever crossed your mind?

I well remember when my thoughts were consumed by past failures and the possibility of facing a lifeless future. I remember the strange mixture of shame and guilt I experienced while at my lowest moments.

I well remember the bad decisions that wreaked havoc on my life. I remember the difficulty in separating facts from emotion, perception from reality, the wheat from the chaff.

I well remember how I financially lost everything while chasing what turned out to be virtually nothing. Quite possibly you know where I have been because you, too, have found yourself there.

After numerous setbacks, the tendency is for something within us to give up and crumble, isn't it? Yet no one can truly understand why we hit this point unless they have been in the same position.

On many occasions, I asked myself, *Do I have the right tools in my mental and psychological toolbox to endure again?* Although the thoughts of quitting were well grounded, giving up was never an option.

There are many paths that lead to success, but only one path that leads to failure. That path is to surrender, to give up, to quit.

The simple fact is that the easiest thing in the world to do is to quit. It takes no talent to throw in the towel or to walk away.

That's not you, is it? Didn't think so. And I am glad it wasn't me.

Fortunately, I didn't lose faith in the belief that there was something better beyond where I was at the time. Several different times I have had to change course, but each time, I was able to emerge on the other side a wiser and stronger person.

I cannot put a price tag on what I learned in those times I was in the valley. The lessons helped me climb back up the mountain again to enjoy many moments of success, happiness, and fulfillment.

But I have often wondered where I would be if I had not been mentally tough and persevered through the tough times. Have you ever been at that place yourself?

Life-Enhancement Message

If you feel in your heart that you have what it takes to be successful in life, then your attitude alone will make up for a great many limitations you might have. But if you don't feel this way, no matter how gifted you are, you won't be consistently successful when facing life's stiffest challenges.

THRIVE OR SURVIVE?

When quitting is not an option, what's next? My personal journey has allowed me to understand how to make the dash more productive and how to weave a fairy tale with the threads of personal goals and dreams despite struggles.

It has been my experience that there is very little difference between the goals and dreams of most of us. We want to do well, to achieve something of significance, to be proud of what we do, to help others improve their lives, to obtain an element of financial security.

Where the difference lies is in how we go about converting these dreams and desires into reality. What do we need to do to make our dash more meaningful and satisfying?

I would assume that you want a life in which you thrive, not one in which you merely survive. I would also presume that you might be searching for ways to improve your ability to have more defining moments in your life. Am I on track?

Hopefully, this book will expose you to life lessons that will elevate the substance of your dash. I am also hopeful that you will be determined enough to not only grasp but apply the ideas that will rewrite your fairy tale. That's what you are looking for, isn't it?

Life-Enhancement Message

Life is not measured by the number of breaths we take, but by the moments that take our breath away.

—Author Unknown

LIVING MORE PRODUCTIVELY

What if you had only one day to live? What would you do on that one day that you don't currently do?

The substance of the latter question is to create a frame of mind in which we are constantly searching for how to live a more meaningful life. But how we accomplish this goal varies from person to person, doesn't it? Do I see you nodding your head?

As we strive to enhance the dash on life's journey, we must create a mind-set that allows us to explore new possibilities, a mind-set that makes us accessible to examining more deliberately the opportunities that life presents to us. It is not the years in life that count, it is the life we put into those years that counts. I hope you hear me saying that life isn't about finding ourselves, it is about creating ourselves.

The one constant in life is its unpredictability. Life is given to each of us on different terms. A great example of this is my wonderful mother, Anna Ruth Vickery. Mother has celebrated ninety-six birthdays. Every day the weather is nice, you will find her working in her garden. We all should be so fortunate.

Mother was the sixteenth child born to William and Emma Wise. That's right, number sixteen. All single births. It is estimated that Mother was born almost three months premature and weighed less than two pounds at birth. This was in 1923, long before incubators and top-notch neonatal care. The doctor told my grandparents that their child would not survive. My grandfather wouldn't buy it. He was determined that he would do everything possible to give his child an opportunity for life. Poppa William created his own incubator for his daughter. He took a big-mouthed gallon jar, packed cotton in the bottom, placed his newborn daughter in the jar, and put a kerosene lantern next to the jar. Daily he would change the cotton in the jar. He and Granny Emma fed Mother with an eyedropper. It was slow going at first, but then she turned the corner and began to grow and develop. Now, here we are all these years later with her still enjoying a quality life.

My grandfather could have taken the doctor's advice and given up, but he didn't. That is a special kind of love, one that every parent and grandparent could take to heart.

My mother was not supposed to have lived. But she did. She was given life—period. And ninety-six years later, she is still making the most of it.

It serves us well to stop once in a while and be thankful for what life has not given us. Most of us know, or have known, someone who has made significant contributions to society despite handicaps and hardships. What internal attributes have allowed them to succeed in overcoming adverse circumstances? How were they able to jump over hurdles and land on success? That is the centerpiece of the time we will spend together in this book.

The antithesis to those who have succeeded in face of adversity are those who live lives of hardship and drudgery despite being right on the cusp of daily opportunities for the enrichment of their lives. They either see or have seen themselves as victims of their circumstances. These individuals have surrendered, given up on life. They didn't perish physically, but they did mentally. Born 1951–Died 2001. They simply gave up on completing the dash in a positive and gratifying way.

There comes a time in the lives of most of us when we come to a fork in the road. Then it becomes decision time. Hall of Fame baseball player and street philosopher Yogi Berra once said, "When you come to the fork in the road, take it!" Which fork, right?

Whichever fork we take will be better than giving up and sitting down in the middle of the road. By sitting there, we are certain to be run over by the future.

Life-Enhancement Message

You will spend your life doing more living when you enjoy where you are on the way to where you are going!

LIVING LIFE WELL

Dr. Ken Blanchard, noted life coach, said, "When we lack progress in life, we have failed to understand how to live life." Sounds reasonable, doesn't it?

The one thing we can count on in life is that it is a laboratory which allows us to continually have opportunities for growth. Life patiently keeps repeating the same lessons until we learn them.

It has been my experience that we live better lives when we keep an eye not just on our standard of living, but also on how we live it. We must not be so preoccupied with making a living that we fail to make our present life worthwhile.

Those who understand the value of living tend to live well. They realize that living is purely in the present, not ahead or behind. While life is understood backward, it unfolds forward. Life is definitely lived in the now.

The wisest move we can make is to choose to live each moment as if that moment was both our first and our last. When we live each moment as it appears, we will always be as young as the present. Beneath life's beautiful wrapper lie the secrets to learning how to take each moment and turn it into a more meaningful and more productive dash.

I really believe a good life depends on depth instead of length. While life isn't tied with a bow, it's still a gift. When we slow down and enjoy the gift, we are able to inhale the best part of life. Make sense?

Make no mistake about it, we have been given life to enjoy living. When we attempt to give more to life than we receive, we will end up receiving more than we give. That's the part so many have failed to understand.

I hope you believe that the best life is one in which you live and help others live, not live and let live. With this kind of attitude, your belief will help make it a reality.

Life-Enhancement Message

The Law of Everything reads, "Everything you do matters. There is no neutrality. For every choice, there is a consequence. That choice will either add value to life or it won't. The decision is yours, and yours alone."

MENTAL TOOLBOX

Have you developed a workable mental toolbox for dealing with life's most challenging situations? Do you have the mental fortitude, the mental acumen, the mental resilience to stand up to the challenges life tosses your way?

I have discovered that there is one constant about a quality mental toolbox: it must be continually upgraded. That is the reason I am offering many strategies in this book for dealing with the varied mental circumstances of life. These strategies offer a clear, confident approach to life situations as they occur. With the right mental tools, we have a good shot of anticipating how things are going to unfold in an unknown future.

A quality mental toolbox also gives us the confidence to keep reaching beyond—seeking, learning, improving, growing. This is how we move beyond "what is" to see where the pockets of greater opportunities may be hiding.

Debra Watson served as one of the content editors for this book. Debra's life fully illustrates the importance of realizing it is not what one comes through, but what one comes to that truly counts in life. Debra told me, "I feel very blessed with my life even though I have had to deal with hardship due to events that occurred very early on." Let's take a look at her childhood.

She and her twin brother were born to her dad's fourth wife. He had a total of seven. They never saw their blood mother again after the age of two. Debra and her older sister and twin brother lived with various relatives, changing locations regularly. They often were malnourished and unkempt.

When her father eventually married his seventh and final wife, Debra was six years old. For the first time in her life, she felt an element of physical stability and safety. But she would be in adulthood before she developed any emotional security. The feeling of abandonment affected Debra and her siblings in different ways. One of the biggest issues facing Debra, as she moved into adulthood, was learning how to trust. Debra found it difficult to trust the feeling that someone could love her unconditionally. Circulating in the back of her mind was the thought that she could be abruptly left. She was afraid of being hurt because she believed that her being was defined by the choices of others.

Debra was in her thirties before she realized that her lack of being able to trust and show vulnerability stunted her ability to develop quality relationships. It stopped her from truly loving, whether it be with a friend or with a partner.

But Debra eventually chose to not let her past experiences dictate her future. She began to believe that her feelings and well-being could actually matter to someone. Debra got married and raised three beautiful daughters. She told me, "There was nothing extraordinary about my adulthood, but I have had a good life."

I think you would agree with me that she had a difficult childhood. But from that adverse beginning, Debra deliberately created a change in her own emotional well-being, and although it took time, her decision allowed her to experience much personal happiness as well as to bring great happiness to others.

I asked Debra what turned things around for her. She said, "Lou, I chose to use my mental resolve to overcome and step beyond what I logically knew robbed me of the most important things in life. It wasn't easy, but through determination and many steps that are described in this book, I feel I altered what could have been easily accepted and ultimately detrimental."

Everyone who aspires to reach a greater level of satisfaction in their lives must do their very best to master every tool in their mental toolbox. I firmly believe that Debra demonstrates how her mental toolset made a difference in her life.

How many quality mental tools do you have in your box? Do you possess the kind of tools that provide the tenacity and mind-set to not only endure life's most challenging moments, but also make you stronger once you have relocated to the other side?

An efficient and workable mental toolbox impacts our lives with every decision we make. It can create and move us right into the midst of greater possibilities. Likewise, the lack of strong mental resolve can rob us of possibilities. A quality mental toolbox can certainly alter the path of any hardship that life has thrown our way.

LIFE IS A GENEROUS GIVER

There is always enough money, time, relationships, love—you name it—available to us. There is virtually an infinite supply of all we need. Do you believe that?

But we have to shift energy toward believing we have the mental fortitude to go after the best that life has to offer. We must come to the realization that life is a generous giver, and life requires nothing more from us than the giving of our best selves.

Deep down in the fiber of our being is the essence of a quality life. The only reason we fail to realize the fairy tale we visualized having is because we haven't established the mind-set to work toward creating that kind of fairy tale.

With the right mental tools, we can actively seek and welcome new experiences. We can even take reasonable and calculated risks that we may never have taken otherwise. This is the type of attitude that will ultimately lead us to the infinite variety of emotions, feelings, and challenges that life has to offer, moment to moment, day to day, year to year. How exciting can that be, right?

Life-Enhancement Message

The only true measure of success is the ratio between what we might have been on one hand and the things we have made of ourselves on the other hand.

—H. G. Wells, Life Coach

LIFE QUESTIONS

I sense that the big wheel in your mind may be turning with thoughts about how well you are doing with your own dash. Am I right?

We will spend the rest of our time in this book providing answers to the questions that help determine the quality of life we experience as we live out the dash. Here are the questions that we will answer together:

- How big a role does fear play in your life? How about stress, anxiety, and pressure?

- How would you describe success and having a successful life? Are you a sincerely happy person?

- How effective are you at letting go and moving on from a bad experience?

- How do you jump-start your future when life's circumstances dictate that adjustments and transformation are needed?

- How do you feel about you? Can you say without reservation that you love yourself?

- Are you continually learning new and better ways to live? Do you have the ability to retrofit yourself in order to make improvements?

- How would you describe your ability to continually learn? Do you find it readily easy to embrace the wisdom of experienced people?

- Do you need some touch-up work on time management and organizational skills?

- Do you possess a rock-solid purpose and crystal-clear vision for moving forward and upward? How good are you at setting goals and using them as motivation to grow and develop?

- How effective are you in preparing yourself for the challenges ahead? Do you have a deep-felt "will to prepare" to succeed?

- Do you readily make choices and decisions that lead to improving your life? Do you have the courage to act on your decisions?

- How tough mentally are you in adapting to the changes happening around you—and within you?

- How's your staying power? Are you effective at putting disappointments and setbacks behind you?

- How good are you at persevering when the odds are stacked against you or things aren't going your way?

- How do you handle it when you royally mess up and are called on the carpet for it? How do you handle the criticism of others?

- What would you say about your character and reputation? Do you do things right because it is right?

- Are life-changers, such as enthusiasm, energy, heart, and faith, a part of your daily life?

- Would you consider yourself an approachable person? What would you say about your overall communication skills?

- Does the Golden Rule rule in your life? How are you functioning in the interdependent world of living with others?

- Is your health your greatest wealth? How are you holding up in the areas of food, exercise, and sleep?

- Are you doing an effective job of handling electronic devices, or are the devices handling you? Is there a possible health issue here?

These are the kinds of questions that tax the intellect and probe the emotions. And these are the kinds of questions we will provide answers for over the pages to come.

So I ask you: Do you possess the mental stamina to face up to these challenges? Do you have the mental fortitude to do your best to establish a renewed attitude so you reach beyond who you are and construct a better dash?

READY . . . SET . . . GROW

Have you been effective and efficient in some parts of your life, but not in others? Do you believe that with a little fine-tuning your life could take on a new significance? Do I sense you agreeing with me?

There are four areas of life—body, brain, heart, and soul—that we will explore together. It takes strength and courage in these four areas for us to move beyond where we are to where we would like to be in life.

Before I get too far along here, I want to place an accent on the next two chapters. They focus on two of the biggest negatives that we face in life: fear and stress. While the thrust of this book is on the positive side, I felt it was best to put these negatives up front. From this base, I believe together we can use them as building blocks to develop something better and stretch beyond to a brighter future.

I want to challenge you to consciously create a mental picture of how the precepts you read about will feel like once achieved. See yourself acting on these life lessons if they are applicable to you. Hear those around you congratulating you on your positive changes. Visualize the desired end result. See yourself stepping out and stepping up, refocusing beyond where you are to seek new and greater possibilities.

When the appropriate feelings and emotions come together, you will make great strides in those areas of your life you desire to im-

prove. Armed with this kind of energy and power, you will bring renewed substance to your life.

Are you ready to awaken the sleeping giant within? Are you ready
to touch your life in a bigger way from all angles? Are you ready to
reach beyond and build a life where the dash will lead to living "happily ever after"?

*The windshield is larger than the rearview mirror for the very
simple reason that life is lived forward, not backward.*

TWO

THE FEAR OF FEAR

Our greatest fear is fear itself!
—President Franklin Delano Roosevelt, 1941

What do you fear? Do you find yourself overwhelmed by thoughts of something that might happen to you? Do you experience difficulty in focusing on anything other than what you are afraid of? Are your fears the primary force behind your decisions and your behavior?

Do you know what I have discovered about fear? Most of us are incredibly unaware of our vulnerability to it. We rarely consciously think about our fears, do we?

There is little question that fear is a real part of our lives, whether we recognize it or not. We become paralyzed by fear that may arise when expected plans go awry, when we receive news that we never wanted to hear, or when we simply conjure up something in the mind that we think might happen to us.

Whatever the cause, when fear gets a foot in the door, it not only paralyzes, it intimidates and debilitates who we are and what we stand for. Fear can ultimately distort our perception of a situation and thereby alter our response.

I truly believe that how we visualize fear has much more of an impact on any situation than the fear itself. The manner in which we choose to look at the consequences of that fear is far more important than the daunting feelings it causes.

I hope this is what you hear me saying: It is one thing to fear, because fear can initially heighten our senses and make us more aware of our surroundings. But it is quite another to let ourselves be led by fear, to let fear develop into the captain of our souls.

I have a family acquaintance who exemplifies how manifesting a fear can not only control every waking hour, but it literally can alter the course of one's life. Let's call her Dorothy Scruggs.

Dorothy is diabetic. She has lost siblings to diabetes. Because of her family background, Dorothy constantly reminds herself, and others, that she will soon be suffering the same fate as three of her brothers and sisters. She is consumed by this thought pattern.

Dorothy has lost her focus on who she currently is. She no longer actively pursues those things that add joy and pleasure to life. Her fear has become her reality. And she is not alone.

What occurs when we keep a fear in the forefront of our minds? It becomes ingrained in our psyche and can create so much legitimacy that it becomes an actuality. Fear then is expressed as something that is specific and definite in our lives. As a result, it expressly changes the characteristics of our behavior.

The pervasive nature of fear leads us to seldom make a conscious effort to acknowledge it, but worse, to not make any meaningful steps to manage it. As a consequence, we lose many precious opportunities to make sufficient steps toward achieving life goals.

When we allow our lives to be controlled by fear, fear becomes our guidance system. It becomes ingrained in our psyche and has so much believability that it becomes second nature.

Since fear resides as an explicit and clear-cut part of our behavior, it becomes the foundation upon which most of our major decisions are made. It is often the barometer of how we perceive life in general. Think about that.

LACK OF UNDERSTANDING

Why do we fail to address the fears that have such devastating control over us? The primary reason is that we lack an understanding of them. We simply struggle to recognize logical reasons for why they exist in the first place.

Even when we are consciously aware of a fear, there is an innate tendency to try to hide it somewhere. This is probably because we are unable to define the origin and specificity that caused the fear to develop in the first place. This shortcoming ultimately leads us to minimize the negative influence fear has on our lives. Because of the lack of specificity about the causes of fear, we tend to relegate fear to the far corners of our being. This is true even when we are consciously aware of a fear. We still have a tendency to try to hide it. "Out of sight, out of mind" results in facing an unknown future filled with undefined fear. We struggle with the inability to make a decisive and rational effort to pinpoint why and what we fear. Consequently, we develop little ammo to combat the angst we experience.

As a professional athlete, I came eyeball-to-eyeball with some form of fear or phobia on a regular basis. How many professions do you know in which your performance is on public display? Your every action is there for all to see. In sports, you are only as good as your last action.

Take my game, baseball. The biggest fear faced by a baseball player is being hit in the head with the ball. This fear is evident at a young age and has kept many young, promising players from continuing to play the game. But you can rest assured that very few would admit that is the reason they quit playing.

It was reported by the media years ago that I probably hold the record for being hit in the head with a baseball in the greatest variety of ways. In fact, I can recall being hit in the head at least twelve different times over the course of my pro career. I was hit by a pitched ball, a hitter's line drive, an umpire's throw (twice), a catcher's throw, while jogging in the outfield, an infielder's throw, by a fan throwing a ball back onto the playing field after it had been hit into the stands, and three times by batted balls while I was off the field of play—including one that ricocheted off a pole and hit me in the back of the head. You find it funny, do you?

I want to share with you one of the times that I was hit with a batted ball while not on the playing field. The story is a mixture of internal pain and external pain, and a touch of humor. Let me explain.

It was my night to be the starting pitcher in a game in Atlanta. In the first inning, I had very little success in getting the Toronto batters out. In fact, I didn't get anyone out before our manager came to the pitching mound and removed me from the game. I headed to the showers.

A book I wrote on baseball in 1995 entitled *Answers to Baseball's Most Asked Questions* (Masters Press, Spalding Books) refers to this as "being knocked out of the box." This is the baseball term for when the manager chooses to replace a pitcher with another pitcher in the course of an inning.

The dressing room in old Ponce de Leon Park, where the game was being played, was down the right-field line past first base. You can imagine the wonderful compliments I received as I made my way toward the runway that led underground to the dressing room.

After a quick shower, I made my way back down the runway to check the scoreboard. Just as I arrived at the entrance to the steps leading to the field, I heard the crack of the bat, signifying that the batter had hit the pitch somewhere. I took a quick glance to see where the ball had been hit.

Unfortunately, that "somewhere" was a foul ball hit directly at me. Understand that the only thing visible in the runway was my head.

Sure enough, the ball hit me squarely between the eyes. Down I went, "knocked out" for the second time during the game. Things had gone from bad to worse very quickly.

No one realized what had happened to me until the ball boy came to retrieve the ball. Soon an ambulance arrived. I was conscious, but with a severe headache, as the ambulance sped away toward Grady Hospital.

After a short ride to the hospital, I underwent a thorough examination of my head. They found out what Mother already knew: I have an extremely hard head.

Other than an earth-shattering headache and a big knot on my forehead, perfectly situated between my eyes, I was okay. I am a great believer that even though the sun has a sinking spell in the evening, it will rise up strong in the morning.

I awoke the next morning with a headache and a bruised ego. But that didn't keep me from grabbing a newspaper and heading to the sports pages.

The sports headline read, "Vickery 'Knocked Out' Twice." But it was the subheading that told the real story: "X-rays of head show nothing." You would not believe the mileage I have gotten out of that statement over the years.

Even when we are consciously aware of a fear, we have a tendency to ignore it, which allows the fear to control some parts of our behavior. As I look back now, I feel that the fear of being potentially hit with a batted ball probably played a role in my pitching pattern. Keep it away from the big hitters, right?

WHAT FEAR MEANS

Fear can be either a noun or a verb. As a noun, fear is an unpleasant or distressing emotion. It is caused by the belief that someone or something is dangerous and likely to cause pain or be a threat. *Being left alone is my greatest fear* is an example of fear being used as a noun.

As a verb, fear is being afraid of someone or something that we believe is likely to be dangerous, painful, or threatening. Terms like *I'm afraid of, fearful of, scared of, dreadful of, apprehensive of, terrified of, anxious about*, and *in horror of* are all verb forms of fear.

Years ago I read this somewhere: "FEAR is an acronym for **f**alse **e**xperiences **a**ppearing **r**eal." This is an excellent description of fear, don't you think? This quote from an unknown source has the ring of truism wrapped all around it.

Experts tell us that we are born with only two innate fears: the fear of loud noise and the fear of falling. That means all the other fears and phobias we experience are learned.

This learning process is so deep and so real that fear becomes an explicit and deep-seated characteristic of our behavior. Fear in essence becomes a real part of our lives. And the manner in which we see a particular fear is more important than the fear itself.

Let's think together here. Do you have something you fear that you do everything possible to avoid? Can you put your finger on it?

ORIGIN OF FEAR

Fears are experienced from infancy to adulthood. The fears experienced in infancy typically grow out of a reaction to something that occurs in the environment.

For instance, I developed a fear of going to the dentist because of the actual pain I experienced during previous dental office visits. Was that an amen I heard from the back of the room?

As we grow older, these fears can broaden and intensify to include various people, imaginary figures, objects, or events.

Some of the other fears we experience are fears of "things," with which we exercise a fight-or-flight response. It is natural for us to react in a fight-or-flight manner to outside stimuli that can bring physical harm.

While we may have the natural instincts to deal with fight-or-flight situations, the same cannot be said for insight. When we are threatened, logic makes a quick exit and emotions take over.

Earlier we talked about how our greatest challenges are internal fears, the ones that originate from within each of us. Because they originate in the mind, it is not the fears that are our biggest concern, it is the thoughts created by the fears.

For example, no one is afraid of heights; they are afraid to fall. No one is afraid to try something new, they are afraid of the unknown that comes with it. No one is afraid of praise and adoration, they are afraid that they won't live up to it the next time. No one is afraid of sticking their neck out, they are afraid they won't like themselves if they are unsuccessful. No one is afraid to play and compete, they are afraid to lose. No one is afraid of the future, they are afraid of what's in it. No one is afraid to reach out and touch someone, they are afraid they will not be touched back. You get the picture, don't you? Thought so.

There is little question that most fears develop from illusory thoughts that become real over time. The more "real" these fears, the larger the role they play in the way we live life.

Although fearful thoughts and feelings arise from something specific that is occurring in the present, they often echo past experiences. They also arise from the anticipation or expectation of a future threat. Regardless of how and when they come up, they are real to us. And as they say, perception is reality.

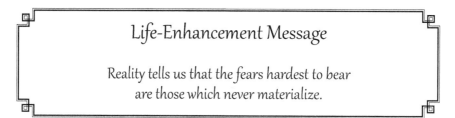

Life-Enhancement Message

Reality tells us that the fears hardest to bear are those which never materialize.

FEAR OF "THEY"

The fear of rejection, like so many of our named fears, has its origin in the fear of "they." To me, this fear is the driving force behind most of what we do. It can be equal parts destructive and constructive. "They" can keep us under the bondage of an unintelligible system. "They" can hold us back from experiencing any measurable degree of success. On the other hand, "they" can be a vital force in being successful. It depends on the situation or circumstances.

Okay, Lou. Who are "they"?

"They" is that gray mass of humanity that surrounds us and that we let manipulate our daily affairs. Because "they" said this or "they" said that, we develop a fear of "they." Our minds love to overgeneralize. If we fear "they" will judge us, think badly of us, or criticize us, we need to ask ourselves exactly who are "they" in our own lives. Name names. Who are the specific people whose opinion you fear? It could be that the urge to fear what "they" think was firmly drilled into your psyche as a child. Think back to your childhood. Was there someone in your family who constantly expressed concern about *What will the neighbors think?* or *We'd better not do that. So-and-so might think badly of us.* Sound familiar?

Acceptance is the golden grail that we cherish. The worst thing to be in this world is "unacceptable" to "they." I can hear you asking, *What is "unacceptable"?* Unacceptable is whatever "they" say it is. "They" say it is unacceptable to live in a poor neighborhood, to not have a lot of money, to be out of style, to drive an old car. "They" determine what we wear, how we speak, our manners, our morality, and even where we go. "They" lay the groundwork for our environment and our society, as a whole. The momentous pressure that is brought on us by "they" magnifies the high premium we pay for acceptance. Like an unseen power, the fear of "they" hypnotizes us to do what we dislike, to go where we don't want to go, to say what we do not believe.

When the opinions of "they" become the centerpiece of our lives, the results are predictable. Like a magnet, "they" pull us down and reduce us to the level of mediocrity.

"They" force us to settle into a set, conventional role. "They" curtail our creativity and individuality. "They" take away our free thought and ability to reason outside of the norm. It is true, when "they" expect a certain thing from us, or for us to act in a certain way, "they" are essentially in charge of our lives. Any move to establish our own identity and face the world with a worthy sense of personal confidence and security goes out the window.

Life-Enhancement Message

To fear "they" is to open the door for the things "they" say to become a reality.

MOVING BEYOND "THEY"

Where does the fear of "they" come from? Is it peer pressure? Insecurities? The desire to be liked? Whatever the source, the result is the same: we open the door for "they" to control our lives. Is the fear of "they" a controlling factor in your life? Is it like a vise with a tight grip on you?

It had definitely been an influence on my life. For a long time, "they" were a constant companion that I kept striving hopelessly to satisfy. Many of my earlier decisions in life were crystalized around the fear of what others would think. "They" were always an invisible party to any decision of consequence that I made. All I could hear was the internal voice reminding me that I needed to focus on what "they" would think and not on what the best decision would be for me. All I could hear was the internal voice reminding me that I needed to focus on what "they" would express, regardless of what I did.

There finally came a time when I realized that, in trying to keep up with "they," I had no time to live life on my terms. For the most part, I found the strength and courage to overcome the insecurities that led to my fear of "they." The turnaround started with a pair of white shoes. Up to that point, I had been overconscious about what others thought of the way I dressed. I would ponder the selection of what to wear with one thought in mind: *What will others think?* I would suspect that a lot of us make clothing choices based on what others might think, don't we?

One night, I was scheduled to speak in Milwaukee. I was running a bit late and had to hustle to get dressed. I had my best Sunday three-piece, dark blue suit with me. I had everything on except my shoes. When I looked in my shoe bag, nothing was there but a pair of white shoes I had worn at a casual gathering on my last trip. I had worn my athletic shoes on the flight up. There was not enough time to locate a shoe store to purchase a new pair. I was left with a choice between white shoes and athletic shoes. The white shoes won.

I decided not to tell the story to my audience about why I was wearing the white shoes with a three-piece suit. Much to my surprise, the shoes were the hit of the night. I received many favorable comments about them after my speech. Some people even expressed that they wished they had the guts to wear what they wanted to without being fearful of what others would think. I learned an important lesson through a pair of white shoes. That incident put me on the road to place the fear of "they" in the rearview mirror.

Do you need to establish your own campaign to manage this life-cramping adversary called "they"? The good news is, whatever fearful beliefs we learned from "they," we can unlearn them. With time and patience, we can replace negative thoughts with something like *They are too concerned with their own lives to care very much about what happens in mine.*

Giving up allegiance to "they" begins with recognizing the mental distortions in life that "they" have brought to the table. If "they" control any part of your life, once you understand the source, you can deal with it. Then you can develop the inner strength to optimize hope and move beyond being a slave to "they." It begins with awareness. It ends with action.

MANAGING OVERALL FEAR

Our efforts to manage fear depend on the answer to the question *What am I hiding with my fears?* Hidden in every fear is a motive for the birth of that fear.

As each fear grows, it insinuates itself deeper and deeper into our psyche, making it tougher and tougher to manage. The longer the fear is left uncontrolled, the more control we will need to manage it. Let me emphasize again: Fear is born from within. Fear must be controlled from within.

What I am saying is that because fear is learned, it can be unlearned. The biggest detriment we have to managing any fear is grasping the threat behind the fear. Once we understand the root cause, we can effectively approach it with an ability to overcome it.

How then do we move on beyond a fear? The following steps can help.

STEPS FOR MANAGING FEAR

1. **Acknowledge.** Admit to yourself that a fear is affecting your life in a very adverse manner. Then get fired up about your willingness to do something about it. Look at the things the fear is robbing you of. That is the beginning of the process of managing it.

2. **Evaluate.** Make a conscious, concerted effort to evaluate the hidden nature of a fear. From this base, you can begin to de-

velop the kind of backbone and game plan needed to confront it. Break it down into parts and look at it objectively.

3. **Explore options.** What options are available to you to mollify the fear? What are the different tools or methods you can use to eradicate this emotion that alters your life? Use your awareness of the fear to extract the ways in which you can learn to suppress it.

4. **Take action.** Ralph Waldo Emerson gave us some sound advice when he said, "Do the things you are afraid to do, and the death of fear is certain." Imagine yourself doing what you fear. Mentally project yourself doing it; feel the reality of it in your imagination. Regardless of the fear, it is always bigger than reality.

Life-Enhancement Message

Today is the oldest you have ever been, yet the youngest that you will ever be, so every day you don't confront fear is one less day you can.

BEING COURAGEOUS

"Courage is not the lack of fear, it is the conquest of it."—William H. Danforth

The opposite of fear is said to be courage. Fear is a mind-set. Courage is an action. Let me share with you a story that demonstrates courage in action.

Janet Perez Eckles was a guest on my radio show many times over the years. Janet is full of life. She exudes a vivacious personality, laughing and talking easily with people from all walks of life. But Janet will never look into her husband's eyes again. She will never see the smile on her children's faces. She won't see her grandchildren change as they grow up. She won't ever again get to see the beautiful leaves change in autumn.

You guessed it: Janet is physically blind. She lost her eyesight at age thirty-one. On top of that, she had to endure pain and grief from the murder of her youngest son.

Janet could easily have drowned in self-pity, anger, and resentment. She chose instead to live with valor and hope and to focus on what she could do to help others. That she has done. Without sight, Janet inspires with her great insight. As a keynote speaker worldwide, Janet has taught thousands of people through her talks to see the best of an authentic life.

Coping with blindness was not easy for Janet. She faced the fear of a life of despair. But Janet's faith and courage intensified and enabled her to put away fear and regret, and focus on a future of service. Blindness sparked Janet Perez Eckles's passion to assist others with their fears and struggles. She has helped move their focus away from hopelessness, toward renewing their vision of lifetime dreams.

There is little doubt that Janet demonstrates acting with courage. She convinced herself that blindness was no excuse for not being an active participant in life.

A STEP OF FAITH

When our fear comes from a place of insecurity in ourselves, or uncertainty about the future, courage may not always be the answer. What happens when our search for courage turns up empty-handed?

Could the ultimate answer to managing fear be found in faith? In chapter 16, there is a beautiful story of how a young lady has used her faith to fight the fear of cancer. Responding to the challenge of fear through faith does strengthen our resolve going forward. Faith moves us beyond fear when doing nothing appears safer.

It is probably easier for us to gauge what faith looks like. Faith helps us to stand tall, where before our fear indicated we should fall. Faith endures in spite of the uncertainty and confusion created by fear. Faith refuses to compromise convictions, even if that means going against "they." Faith offers steadiness where fear has caused us doubt and hopelessness. Faith helps us remain strong where fear would sap our energy and enthusiasm. Faith works from the inside out. It changes how we think, as well as how we speak and how we act. Faith is our inner strength in face of fear brought on by opposition, indifference, or division.

One of the most therapeutic things we can use in establishing the kind of faith that will move us beyond fear is found in the power of suggestion. The force of mental suggestion is so great it is often a better cure for physical ills than is modern medicine.

We will never know how to live without fear until we make the internal decision to use our faith to move us beyond fear. With every experience, every effort, and every faith-filled hope, we will get a little closer to removing fear from our lives and bring greater meaning to our dash.

Life-Enhancement Message

Having faith in the future is an important part of
creating a future worth having faith in.

THREE

THRIVE IN CHAOS

I am often asked, "Lou, what is the biggest single issue an individual faces today?" There are many possible answers, but each contains the same base word—chaos. Chaos is a mixture of stress, pressure, anxiety, and the like. The chaotic nature of today's society is an outgrowth of unprecedented demands to compete and succeed. Accordingly we encounter unrealistic standards that we have never faced before. We will spend our time together in this chapter exploring ways to navigate these unprecedented standards that have created unrelenting stress and pressure.

Here's a great experiment to illustrate how various things differ "under fire." They very well could be indicative of how we differ when the heat is on and action is needed. Take a piece of meat, sand, clay, a piece of wax, and wood, and throw all of them into a fire. Now, how do you suppose they react? The meat fries, the sand dries up, the clay hardens, the wax melts, and the wood burns. Every one of these items was subjected to the same external condition—the fire—yet all reacted differently.

Under identical conditions, we are like the articles in the fire, we react in different ways. Some of us may become stronger, while others may become weaker. Some may do nothing; some may jump in with both feet. It will depend on our individual makeup, won't you think?

How do you react to chaos? What can you say about your ability to thrive in chaos? Do you need a tune-up for dealing with the chaotic circumstances of stress and its two siblings, anxiety and pressure, which can arise in virtually all facets of life?

DISTRESS OF STRESS

Stress is a by-product of fear. Think about it: If we had no fears, we would have no need to stress about anything, would we? We allow ourselves to become uptight over finances, careers, health, relationships, and a ton of smaller, less significant areas of our lives, don't we?

We all know that life would be lived far more productively and joyfully if there was no stress in our lives. But that's just not realistic, is it?

Earlier in my life, I often heard the saying "If you can't stand the heat, stay out of the kitchen." Rarely does anyone reach the pinnacle of success without experiencing some mayhem along life's way. The presence of the chaotic side of stress tends to intensify because of the anticipatory nature of what lies ahead.

How do you react in the midst of a stressful situation? Does your heart begin to pound more than normal? Do your palms become sweaty? Does a big lump develop in your throat? Do you have doubts that you can meet the stressful situation head-on and create the outcome you desire?

It has been my experience that chaotic situations brought on by stress can either bring out the best in us or the worst. Since stress is ultimately a part of life, the natural goal would be to lessen it so it has minimal control over our affairs. It simply depends on how we go about managing it.

EFFECTS OF STRESS

Stress for most of us is a negative force. We tend to internalize it. When absorbed inwardly, stress retards our ability to operate at peak performance. It has a negative impact on our actions by producing distinct physiological changes in the mind and body. For starters, inward stress limits reaction time. Blood vessels constrict, which reduces the supply of blood to the brain, affecting our ability to think clearly.

Concentration is affected, limiting our ability to stay focused. The results are predictable: we perform at a level that is far below what we are capable of doing.

But there is also a brighter side to stress. Some stress is essential to our well-being. Stress can be a positive force when its power is exerted outwardly. Stress is not, after all, what happens to us. It is how we react to what happens to us.

I am quite certain that the right level of stress handled in the right way carries awesome potential. It can bring depth and meaning to our daily activities. It can provide greater motivation toward performing at an optimal level. Stress assures the presence of vitality, zest, and a sense of challenge. When you encounter stress, do not fixate on the tension that can keep you from effectively managing the situation. Think instead of how the stressful condition can be an incentive to move you forward toward the emergence of a better outcome.

Life-Enhancement Message

Do your best in less critical situations so you can learn how to respond with a higher sense of purpose in more demanding situations.

THE ALMIGHTY DOLLAR

All of my adult life I have heard the expression "Money can't buy happiness." Although that may be true, a serious lack of it can definitely "buy" hardship. I would venture that the money issue is or has been the greatest source of chaos in the lives of most of us.

Our dependency on financial security to alleviate the stress in our lives is well documented. We are happy when we have it and stressed out when we don't.

My question to you is, How much money do you actually really need? Like most of us, you need "enough," right? But what is enough? I believe you will know it when you see and feel it. And that will be different from person to person, won't it?

There is nothing written in stone—no consensus—on what money actually does to satisfy an inner void. It doesn't always deliver any lasting meaning to our lives. Money is a means to an end, not an end in itself.

There is little question that the financial side of life plays a significant role in our health and well-being. It is my conviction that greater financial peace can be a by-product of the life lessons in this book. If we have the mental fortitude to follow through on the lessons we will share together, the money issue will tend to resolve itself.

NONPRODUCTIVE DEFENSE MECHANISMS

We have seen that stress can affect us in both positive and negative ways. Now let's take a look at what defensive mechanisms do to most of us who use them to cope with stress. Unfortunately, the majority of them are not very productive.

For example, if we are hard workers, we tend to work harder. If we mostly blame others for our problems, we will intensify the blame of others. If we are bent toward sweeping things under the rug, we will deny things with even greater force. If we have a dependent nature, we will tend to lean even more heavily on others.

As long as these defenses are employed, we learn nothing constructive about how to handle stress. We just continue to use our prevailing reactions without actually creating something that could lead to a more positive outcome. We also reinforce our nonproductive and familiar defensive mechanisms. This bag of psychological tactics will not benefit us or the situation at hand.

It takes courage to admit that something may be amiss, that stress, pressure, and anxiety are tangible negatives in our lives. But isn't the reduction of these negatives one of the things courage is for? Once we accept this fact, we can then use our courage to reduce the negatives and seek something more effective.

MANAGING CHAOS

There is one thing for sure: managing chaos is purely something that comes from within us. We can learn, practice, and develop personal thoughts, beliefs, and strategies for instinctively building chaos-related defenses. During my professional-baseball-playing days, I learned a few important lessons about dealing with stress and pressure. None were more important than these:

- One play is never more important than another play.
- One game is never more important than another game.
- The first contest of the season is just as important as the last.
- There are no pressure situations, only situations in which we feel or experience pressure.

Translate these important lessons in your daily affairs, notably the last one. There is no question in my mind that the most demanding form of mental discipline is needed when the chips are down and the rewards are high. This may vary from task to task or job to job, depending on your personal situation. But I assure you that, whatever you do, you will experience some pressurized moments. Doing anything worthwhile always comes with stress.

Yet why is it that when right on the brink of making a key decision or experiencing a life-changing moment, some individuals flinch, retreat, or lose courage at the very moment that it is most needed? What keeps these individuals from hanging tough when the stress level is high?

I remember, in my years as a professional baseball pitcher, hearing comments all the time like "Stop thinking and just pitch," "Relax out there; you're thinking too much," and "Concentrate more on the pitch."

When we are told to concentrate or focus, what do we concentrate on? Does the thought of what others are saying creep into your mind and override all other thoughts? Are you more worried about making a mistake or miscalculation than your next effective action? If we have to force ourselves to concentrate, that's where our focus is, isn't it? It is certainly not on the task before us.

What I am saying is I haven't found any absolute formulas for managing the chaotic situations created by stress and pressure. But

I do believe that *focus* holds the key. I have discovered that the ability to focus on the execution of the task we are performing—not on what the result of the execution might be—leads to a more satisfying conclusion The execution of a task is more powerful when we have built a mental focus that is permanently *maintained* on a task, not one in which the focus is *attained* now and then. In other words, a steady focus will always exceed a wavering one

Life-Enhancement Message

Successful results tend to come to those who have come to realize that when their focus is on the "now" moment, they may not always be right in a "pressure" situation, but they will not be fearful of being wrong.

BUCKLE YOUR CHINSTRAP

Okay. What are our plans for dealing with fear, stress, anxiety, pressure—the negatives that bring chaos to our lives? I would venture that all of us have, at times, let these negatives grip our lives, hindering our opportunities for developing a more productive life. Some of us have even been brought to our knees because of the difficulties created by these chaotic burdens.

The weight of these burdens hampers productivity and peace of mind. Many of us have wrestled earnestly with them in such a way that we have either considered giving up or have given up on something that was important to our growth and betterment.

The last thing most football players physically do prior to a play on the field is to buckle their chinstrap. Sometimes it is important to take stock and make certain we are buckling our chinstrap to tackle the things that bring chaos to our lives.

Thoughts influence actions and actions influence thoughts. This never-ending cycle makes it evident that the presence of chaos brought on by stress, pressure, and anxiety is virtually 100 percent mental. This would then indicate that it is virtually 100 percent manageable.

Handling chaos is, in my estimation, all wrapped up in our mental approach. The key is to arm ourselves with a mentally tough approach, one that views the negatives that create chaos as challenging and exciting, rather than overwhelming and daunting.

Thriving in the chaos means we have positioned ourselves to be ready to grow beyond the negatives and to grab hold of something that brings marked improvement to our approach toward life. Life is definitely tough enough without making it tougher, don't you think?

The ability to thrive in chaos greatly depends on putting the accent on the positive things that can arise from chaos. For right in the middle of every chaotic situation that puts a hold on living life with gusto and with purpose is a solution to make life better and more enjoyable. Going forward with our journey, the accent will be on the positive things. Are you ready?

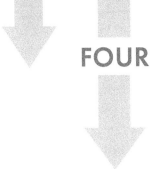

FOUR

THE ROAD TO SUCCESS

Before you can pursue success,
you need to understand what it is and what it isn't.
—Alex Jasin

I hope you have realized by now that this book has one goal: to facilitate a more successful and happy dash. We all want to enjoy a successful life. We also want to experience happiness along the way.

Enjoying success at what we do doesn't always guarantee happiness. Success is arriving at a place in life where our goals and personal victories have been met. Happiness is a place in our minds where we are gratified with where we are and what we have.

So why wouldn't being successful make us happy if we have reached our goals? Because happiness is a state of mind that is created as we travel the road to success. It is something we hold in our hearts, not necessarily something we can hold in our hands.

What do most people do in their desire to achieve success and happiness? They chase all the worldly trappings: money, fame, power. Most never slow down enough to ask one essential question: *What actually are success and happiness to me?*

We will tackle the happiness question in the next chapter. For now, let's look at this thing called *success.*

It is very unproblematic to define success in sports. Winning and losing are straightforward, as the scoreboard tells the story.

In life, that distinction is not quite as simple, is it? So what do we mean when we talk about a successful dash?

It is my conviction that what we consider to be a sufficient level of success is very much a personal thing. Some of us measure it by material growth; others by internal sensitivities. I like to think that it is a combination of the two.

Check out these statements from various unknown sources on their take on success and experiencing a successful life:

"A successful life depends more on what we become than on what we acquire."

"The things that count the most in a successful life are the things that only each individual can count."

"Success is inward, not outward. It depends on what you made of yourself, not on what you have acquired for yourself."

"The real opportunity for success lies within the person and not the job."

"Success is measured by doing something you love and enjoying it while you are doing it."

Okay, after reading those statements, how would you define success? What I get from these statements is that success is both a goal and a journey. When we reach a goal we feel successful, don't we? But we don't stop there, do we? We keep pushing toward another goal. We strive for more and are constantly attempting to improve upon the level that we have already attained.

In a previous book entitled *Traveling Tips along Success Road* (Upword Press, 2008), I wrote:

SUCCESS IS not everything, but striving to be a success is. It is having a badge of honor of doing your best, giving the most you have, being productive to the peak of your capacity.

SUCCESS IS mentally painting big pictures and then working hard and smart to turn those pictures into reality.

SUCCESS IS setting stretch goals and working relentlessly toward their accomplishment.

SUCCESS IS adopting a code of conduct of high standards of thought and behavior and holding these standards as sacred without succumbing to pressure to change them.

SUCCESS IS holding the belief that to receive something you must give something, and the giving always comes first.

SUCCESS IS appreciating that success is something you experience on the inside, not something you have on the outside. It is measured by what you hold in your heart, not in your hands.

SUCCESS IS equipping yourself with the acumen and discernment to capably make wise choices and decisions wherever you are and at whatever you are doing.

SUCCESS IS always being thankful for what you have, then setting out to do your best to make it better.

SUCCESS IS the belief that to count as something special to others, you must first count as something special to yourself.

SUCCESS IS making every effort to move forward as if the limits of what you are capable of doing do not exist.

SUCCESS IS not something you find; it is something you create one task, or even one thought, at a time. And the more comfortable you become with success, the easier it becomes to achieve success.

SUCCESS IS having a motivation of your own choosing—of always doing what is truly "you," and putting every ounce of your being in doing it to the best of your ability.

SUCCESS IS winning the battle in the greatest contest you will ever face—*the contest within yourself.*

A good, honest evaluation is well worth every minute to ensure we are on the right road to success and internal prosperity. We should be asking ourselves the following questions to help determine if we are on the right path:

- Can I clearly envision the success I am striving for?

- Where have I already been successful in my life?

- What do I need to nurture and cultivate to continue building on that success?

- What type of lifestyle do I want to have going forward while pursuing success?

- What steps do I need to take to achieve the level of success to which I aspire?

- What have I learned about minimizing my weaknesses and maximizing my strengths?

- Do I seek feedback from those around me who will provide objective assessments?

- Can I specifically define the areas where I need to be mentally tough to overcome any obstacles?

There is one thing we can count on for sure: the road to success runs right through each of us. That means the only person who can keep you from greater success is you.

PERSONAL SABOTAGE

Let me ask you a couple of straightforward questions. Do you feel that you are sometimes your own worst enemy? Do you have a tendency to sabotage opportunities for greater success in your life?

There are some who create snags of their own making. They believe, for assorted reasons, that they should not be, or have not earned the right to be, successful. As a consequence, they find a way to sabotage any potential success they might experience. Just about the time they find themselves on the verge of being successful, they stick a pin in it. Ultimately, they don't get the successful ending they want because they won't allow themselves to have it. They give every indication that they have a fear of being successful.

I often saw this in athletics. There were those who had the talent to be highly successful, yet succumbed to an inner fear that they were not worthy of success. They didn't say it out loud. The evidence was in the results.

Take Harry Warner (a fictitious name) for example. He could throw a baseball as hard as anyone in pro baseball at the time. We were teammates for two seasons. After Harry had a very successful second season in the minor leagues, he was on the verge of making it to the big leagues, but he came to Spring Training the next season badly out of shape.

Harry didn't handle his breakout season very well. He wasn't mentally prepared to build on it. He often expressed, "I can't believe I'm on the doorstep to the major leagues!" Harry dedicated so much of his life to training to be exactly at the place he wanted to be and for the opportunity that he dreamt of. But once there, he decided he didn't deserve it and unconsciously destroyed it. I think his disbelief affected his preparation. Unfortunately, an injury to his pitching shoulder soon ended his career, and Harry would never have the same opportunity again.

The road to success is built on the platform of mental fortitude and stability. Mental toughness is never needed more than when we face the battles to overcome self-placed hurdles that keep us from being more successful.

The level of success that we experience is equal to the determination we exhibit when building upon the success we have. And as established earlier, there is only one person who can keep you from a more successful life, and that is you.

AN ATTITUDE TOWARD RESULTS

What is your attitude toward results? It is highly important to success that you have a healthy, ongoing attitude toward obtaining the results you desire. Each time we anticipate that we can obtain quality results, the brain is treated to an injection of dopamine, the chemical that makes us look forward to repeating winning experiences.

Remembering those times that we achieved goals, regardless of how insignificant, helps us do two things: it counteracts the self-defeating thoughts that keep us from seeing future progress and recalling even our small wins, and it helps us confidently persist when roadblocks are in our way.

If we enter a task with a healthy results-oriented attitude, that is the direction in which our efforts will take us. We tend to see opportunities where others fail to see them. We get through and over obstacles that stop less successful people. When we focus energy on the kind of results we want and expect, we are more apt to find the resources necessary for acquiring them. Our attitude toward results influences our actions and expectations of attaining them.

Never underestimate the importance your attitude toward results plays in obtaining them. Results are the accumulation of your thoughts, attitude, and efforts. Results are the ultimate barometer by which all of these things are measured.

Life-Enhancement Message

High achievers focus little energy on what could keep them from performing up to their capabilities. They stay focused on what is needed to get the job done—they focus on finding the resources they need to achieve successful results.

EXCELLENCE IS GOOD ENOUGH

Do you expect perfection from yourself? I have found that those who expect perfection are the ones who spend significant valuable time thinking up excuses for why things get off track or searching for ways to cover up their mistakes. Perfection is something to shoot for, but somewhere along the line most of us learn that things rarely come off as planned. Untimely things happen.

When things go wrong do you tend to get upset because your performance was less than perfect? It has been my experience that when things go off course and we become upset, it affects our future course of action. As a good friend once told me, "When things go wrong, don't go wrong with things."

Being successful requires making an effective compromise with perfection. I believe that working toward excellence will suffice.

Now, that doesn't mean that we should relish the thought of being less than perfect. It simply means that one of the biggest mistakes we can make is to not attempt something because we fear that we will be less than perfect.

Look at every challenge you face with an expectation that you will do your very best to be perfect. Then if you fall a bit short, where does that leave you? At the doorstep of excellence, right?

Carry this around with you: You don't have to be perfect to be successful. Excellence is good enough.

HANDLING SUCCESS

I would like to think that after you read this book, you will hasten your journey toward being more successful, that you will feel you have the tools and mind-set to experience more happiness. Can you picture that in your mind's eye?

Since you are going to enjoy a greater measure of success, I want to get this on the table right now: One of the biggest challenges faced by those who enjoy a higher measure of success doesn't come from others, it comes from within. It comes from learning how to handle success.

I have no doubt that you will be able to manage your greater success. But you must realize that the one thing all successful people must learn is the ability to live with the achievements they have earned.

After you have achieved a certain degree of success, it's easy to settle into a routine that is comfortable. But that comfort can be very short-lived. We have explored that past success is important to future success because it helps us build the confidence we need to achieve current goals. But we must be careful not to spend too much time looking at yesterday's achievements, or we may fail to challenge ourselves enough today.

The most successful people are always pushing forward and expanding boundaries. A great example of this is Hall of Fame professional football player George Blanda.

George played professional football for twenty-six seasons, the most in sports history. Early in his career, he was both a highly effective quarterback and an accurate placekicker. After Blanda was no longer able to be effective as a starting quarterback, he became a backup quarterback and remained a highly efficient kicker. He scored more points than anyone in the history of pro football at the time of his retirement in 1976 at the age of forty-eight.

I met George Blanda after his career had ended. Coach Bum Phillips, a former professional coach with the Houston Oilers and New Orleans Saints and a business associate of mine, introduced me to George.

The three of us—Bum, George, and I—had a wonderful visit over a long lunch of Texas barbecue. The conversation ultimately settled on the pro football season of 1970, which was Blanda's twenty-third year in pro football. After completing so many key passes and kicking so many important field goals and extra points in so many games, Blanda was asked by a sportswriter, "George, out of all the games you have played, which is your favorite?" Without hesitation, George stated these powerful words: "My next one." This was in early October of the Oakland Raiders' 1970 season.

Despite all of Blanda's great achievements, something even greater still lay ahead.

Blanda's five-game stretch in 1970 is as good as it gets in pro football. It began on October 25. Blanda took over for starting quarterback Daryle Lamonica and threw three touchdown passes to lead the Raiders to a victory over the Pittsburgh Steelers. The next week, Blanda kicked a forty-eight-yard field goal to beat the Kansas City Chiefs. He followed that performance by throwing a TD pass with 1:34 left to tie the game, and then kicked the game-winning field goal with three seconds remaining as the Raiders defeated the Cleveland Browns 23–20. The fourth week, George threw a twenty-yard TD pass to Fred Biletnikoff against the Denver Broncos with 2:28 left in the game to give the Raiders another come-from-behind victory. The next week, the miracle worker was at it again, as Blanda kicked a sixteen-yard field goal with eight seconds left to beat the San Diego Chargers. George Blanda led the Raiders to first place in the American Football Conference–Western Division that year. At age forty-three, he was the AFC Most Valuable Player.

It was this mentality, this type of mind-set, this type of desire, that drove George Blanda throughout his career. George could have thought when his quarterbacking days were over, *I have done enough. After all, it's more than most have done.* He could have retired. But then the pro football world would have missed out on his miracle year of 1970.

George Blanda did a great job of handling his success. His "my next one" mentality is worthy of being a part of our mental toolbox, don't you think?

Many of those who shared with me their success stories had a commonality in their responses. They struggled initially with finding firm footing before establishing a successful base. It has been my experience that anything truly worthwhile is at first difficult. For example, Randy Owens, of the musical group Alabama, once told me that it took the group ten years to become an "overnight sensation." But once these achievers got a handle on things, they begin to experience consistent success. They also realized that it took just as much energy and focus to stay there as it did to get there.

SUCCESS LEAVES CLUES

Regardless of where we are on the success ladder, we can never afford to rest on our laurels. A truth of life is that those with more drive and ambition will knock us right off our pedestal if we do.

Success can be easily lost unless we are deliberately aiming higher, breaking through new barriers, learning new and better ways to perform, striving to enjoy better results today than we did yesterday, and constantly attempting to improve our body of work.

What do you need to do to continue the climb up the success ladder in the fashion you would like? Success always has built-in clues as to what you need to do to continue along that path. There are lessons in success, just as there are in failure. The key is to look at success as a building block. There are always clues in success that help improve the process to further success. Sound reasonable?

Just for the record, please understand that success is never final. Neither is failure.

ATTAINING SUCCESS IS . . .

ATTAINING SUCCESS IS a challenge—accept it.
ATTAINING SUCCESS IS an adventure—dare it.
ATTAINING SUCCESS IS an opportunity—take it.
ATTAINING SUCCESS IS a mystery—unfold it.
ATTAINING SUCCESS IS demanding—face it.
ATTAINING SUCCESS IS a puzzle—solve it.
ATTAINING SUCCESS IS a risk—undertake it.
ATTAINING SUCCESS IS a goal—achieve it.
ATTAINING SUCCESS IS an experience—enjoy it.
ATTAINING SUCCESS IS a mission—fulfill it.

—Adapted from an unknown author

FIVE

THE PURSUIT OF HAPPINESS

Have you ever said to yourself, *When I get that new job, that raise, a new relationship, a bigger house more success, then I'll be happy*?

If this is the way you think, my news for you is not good. You are, in the words of a songster, "looking for happiness in all the wrong places."

Many people who have worked and struggled to reach the pinnacle of success feel miserable and unhappy when they get there. They are unhappy because they pursued the wrong kind of success—one that didn't match their values. Unless the pursuit of happiness is based on our value system, then happiness will be just another word in our vocabulary. It will be a meaningless thought with no substance.

I have learned that one of the chief sources of unhappiness is the continual search for happiness. Happiness is a by-product of the journey along life's path. It is the result of living a life true to ourselves. It's not an external place we build, it's an internal place we discover.

What I mean is happiness is something we find, not something we create. When desperately sought, it is rarely ever found.

Another way to look at happiness is that it is akin to chasing a butterfly. If we go at a butterfly in a direct fashion, it simply flutters off in a different direction, doesn't it?

As you look at your life right now, can you say you are a truly happy person? If not, what would it take for you to increase the happiness factor in your journey through life?

I am a firm believer that happiness does not arise from monumental events. It is found in the countless little pleasures and small wonders we enjoy each day. It is the small things that work their way down through the creases and grooves to settle quietly into the corners of our hearts.

We all have or are doing something that can be a source of happiness. I know I have had times when enjoyment was hard to find. Quite possibly you have, too. But the elements of happiness were always there. We just lost sight of them.

Life-Enhancement Message

A beautiful part of being human is recalling life experiences that have forged themselves as memories in the alcove of our hearts. Some of these memories bring a smile or chuckle. Others conjure up thoughts that are not very pleasant. But our happiest memories are those that seep out of our eyes, stream down our cheeks, and settle gracefully on the future. They provide a sign of hope for what tomorrow may bring.

THE HAPPINESS QUEST

If you took the time to adjust your happiness factor, where would you start to look for what needs retuning? A joyless job? A bad relationship? An unhealthy habit? A sense of bitterness? A harmful grudge?

For some the list of things that lead to unhappiness could fill several pages. What would your list look like? What would be your top priority to fix? Would you know what needs to be tackled first? What are the things that you truly do not enjoy doing or wish you could quit doing? What kind of mental resolve do you need to bring improvement to those parts of your life?

It is imperative that we first discover and then focus on those things that allow us to find happiness. When we focus on and appreciate the good things in life, they will grow and make life a happier place to be.

Again, our mind-set can make all the difference in how we perceive the good around us. I hope you can wrap your hands around that component of truth.

Look at these additional thoughts on happiness:

- Happiness is found in the size of our gifts, not in the size of our possessions. It doesn't come from what we receive from others; it comes from what we unselfishly give.

- Happiness is inward, not outward. It is not what is around us, but what is in us; it is not what we have, but what we are that is our greatest source of happiness.

- Happiness is knowing that the feeling we have toward what we have is the right feeling, and once we get the hang of being happy, it is a hard habit to break.

- Happiness costs nothing. It's priceless, but only if we can see its value.

- Happiness is present tense, not future tense. If you can't find happiness in what you are doing right now, you will find it difficult to be happy at any time, under any conditions. Remember, it's a state of mind, not a state of events.

Over the years, I have found there are three secrets to happiness:

1. Something—or someone—to love
2. Something to enjoy doing
3. Something to look forward to

Life-Enhancement Message

Someone who is happy and appears to be above worldly concerns is referred to as being "on cloud nine." The term comes from the altitude of clouds. Cloud types are numbered by altitude from one to nine, meaning the highest altitude carries a rating of nine. How often do you have a cloud-nine experience?

HAPPY FOLKS

This is an excerpt from a book I did over thirty years ago, entitled *Up Your Attitude*. I updated a few points, but for the most part, the message is intact.

Happy folks are healthy folks. They are not happy because they are healthy. They are healthy because they are happy. It is the unhappy folks who fill up the hospital beds.

Happy folks have a sense of humor. They have learned to laugh at themselves as well as with others. They don't take themselves too seriously. They know laughter is great medicine for lifting themselves up when they are down.

Happy folks enjoy people. They have a sincere concern for others. They get to know people and let others know them. And it's when they benefit others that they experience a greater happiness within themselves.

Happy folks take things as they come. They don't stew over situations they can't do anything about. They accept things as they are and get on with doing something about those things they can control.

Happy folks put out positive vibes wherever they are. They are grateful for what they have, excited about where they are and what they are working on, and hopeful about the possibilities of the future.

Happy folks understand the value of money. They realize money alone will not bring happiness, but it's certainly a down-payment. On a more serious note, money was meant to serve, not be a master.

Happy folks are those who know the value of living in the here and now. They do ñot concern themselves with what has happened in the past. They have learned how to live in the moment and make the most of what's in front of them now.

Happy folks enjoy themselves. They have a high regard for their own self-worth. They enjoy being themselves, and they recognize that the only true happiness they will ever have originates in the deepest part of themselves.

Happy folks know they will find themselves in some deep water once in a while. But they don't sink. They work deliberately and quickly to get themselves out, and they work to stay out.

Happy folks have discovered that they can't simply act happy. They have to truly be happy. And they are.

ATTITUDE OF GRATITUDE

Are you grateful for the special people you have in your life? Do you freely express your gratitude to them for the way they make your life even more worthy of living? Learning to be thankful for those who are an important part of our lives is more than simply being thankful for what they do for us. It positions us to both give and receive abundant blessings.

Do you realize how much expressing feelings of gratitude to others adds to the quality of our own lives? That's right. The more we show our thankfulness, the more we are connected to a brighter future.

Do you make a concerted, consistent effort to be appreciative of the good things others do for you? Today you are going to have many opportunities to show your appreciation to those who add pleasure to your life. Will you seize upon those opportunities of gratefulness? Will you react positively to the good they bring your way? Will you appreciate the deeds done for you, regardless of how small? Will you simply say, "Thank you!"?

Thank you are two priceless words. They cannot be bought or sold. They are born out of sincerity and are an expression of an authentic person. The thank-yous we send out not only enrich the lives of others, but, like a boomerang, they return to add richness to our lives as well.

A significant amount of happiness flows from an "attitude of gratitude." Being grateful allows many positive feelings to flow into and through our lives. An ever-present gratefulness leads to us living a life with many happy moments. Is there any doubt that being grateful is one of the greatest feelings we can experience in life? How good is your ability to recognize and then vocalize your appreciation to others for what they do for you?

Fellowship and relationship-building emanate from two words: *Thank you.* Just to hear these words creates a clear, beautiful, and positive feeling.

Life-Enhancement Message

Being grateful should be a reaction from the heart more than from the wallet.

GRATEFULNESS AIDS HEALTH

I hope you're ready for this one. Do you believe offering and receiving words of appreciation make for a healthier brain and body? The feelings of gratitude we experience or provide create an ever-increasing sense of well-being. Studies have proven that gratefulness enhances health.

Those of us who feel thankful and regularly express gratitude tend to appreciate our health more. This leads us to take better care of ourselves, and as a result, we feel more energetic and full of life.

Gratitude helps us sustain a high-energy thought pattern that connects us to the best that life has to offer. The grateful mind tends to focus on the best, and therefore attracts the best.

Possessing an attitude of gratitude helps us be more resilient, too. By being constantly aware of the kind acts of others, we tend to look for the positive in almost any situation. This makes it easier for us to overcome the trauma of a bad experience or occurrence.

Are you mindful enough to reflect upon your present blessings and be grateful for what you have? We all have many blessings that we can be thankful for, and when we focus on them and not on our past misfortunes—of which we all have had some—we feel better about ourselves and our circumstances.

It was Zig Ziglar who reminded us that "gratitude is the healthiest of all human emotions. The more you express gratitude for what you have, the more likely you will have even more to express gratitude for." And I might add, the more gratefulness we express, the more worthiness we have as human beings.

When we acknowledge things with an attitude of gratitude, our mood and perspective take on a whole new aura of positiveness. The gratefulness element keeps us keenly aware of the value of others in shaping our lives. Being thankful for what we have, regardless of how little it might be, opens the door for greater conditions to prevail in our lives. An attitude of gratitude will definitely improve our altitude.

Think about these words:

> By relying on others as they do on you,
> You see how interdependent we all are too;
> And why it is an important and worthy goal,
> To take time to say "thanks" for others' role.

BE AMONG THE GIVING

I spent the winter of 1969–70 in New York City. I was there attending training classes for a new position with Merrill Lynch. Each weekday, I rode the subway to downtown Manhattan and back. I was living on the west side of Central Park, which meant I had to change trains at

Grand Central Station. One afternoon on my way home, as I exited the train at Grand Central Station, there was a lot of commotion on the exit platform. I could hear a woman screaming, "Get away from him; he's gone mad!" The crowd appeared to back away in unison.

My eyes immediately viewed a man lying on the concrete platform having an epileptic grand mal seizure. When I arrived the man was experiencing severe convulsions, resulting in his body moving in varied directions on the ground. I immediately recognized what was going on because of previous training in college. I rushed to the man's side to stabilize his bouncing body and keep him from falling onto the train tracks where the power lines would result in electrocution.

The man's head was constantly banging on the hard concrete. I quickly took my suit coat off and placed it under his head. I removed my wallet from my trousers and placed the corner of it into his mouth to prevent him from swallowing his tongue. As I completed this action, I heard a voice behind say in a forceful tone, "What do you think you are doing?" I turned to look. A policeman was standing behind me. I quickly responded, "I'm saving this man's life." With that answer, I went back to attending to the injured man.

I believe the policeman was cognizant that I knew what I was doing when he asked, "How can I help?"

"Please help me keep him stabilized," I responded.

Shortly, the seizure was over. All this action took place in just a few minutes.

I didn't learn the man's name at the time. The policeman took my name and address, "just for the record," he said.

Several weeks later I received a letter from New York City Mayor John Lindsay thanking me for my actions. Included in the mayor's letter was a statement of gratitude from a Mr. Jacob Goldstein. He was the man who had suffered the seizure. A smile of happiness brushed across my face and warmed my heart.

What made that day, at that moment, so important was that I simply reacted to a need. I wasn't looking for accolades. I had something I could give and I did.

What can we learn from this story? When we are well grounded by a strong heart that nudges us toward serving others in a time of need, we grasp any moment that affords us an opportunity to do just that.

GIVING IS LIVING

Most of the opportunities we have to give will not be as dramatic as the story I just told. Life is full of varied ways to give. But one thing stands out to me: the way we give is more important than what we give.

I hope you can envision the significance of that statement. Add this one to it: We have not truly given until we give away something we think we really need. That would be the epitome of giving, don't you think?

Dr. Billy Graham offered, "We can give without loving, but we cannot love without giving."

I like to think that we live by what we *get*, but we make a life by what we *give*. Likewise, we are happy with what we get, but we are happier with what we give.

There are perilous schemes all around us that will prod us toward being uncaring and self-serving. Here's a good reminder for all of us: when we give hoping that we will receive something in return, we are not really giving, we are bargaining.

Do yourself a favor and read these words slowly: "Give away what you cannot keep, to gain what you cannot lose. For what you keep for yourself, you will eventually lose, but what you give away, you can keep forever"—a great quote from an unknown source.

Life-Enhancement Message

Your level of happiness and the kind of life you will live will be determined by what you scatter, not by what you gather.

SIX

JUMP-START YOUR FUTURE

Do you remember the last time you left a motivational meeting or read a self-help book all fired up to change? You were determined that you were going to make some important adjustments in certain areas of your life that would help to jump-start your future. *This time,* you said, *I'm going to change this or that.* How did it work out for you?

Unfortunately, for most of us, a few days later the internal fire and determination burned out. It was back to life as normal without any concerted effort to make the intended improvements we were so resolved to make. We meant well, but we did little or nothing to actually make adjustments and improvement going forward.

The modifications may need to be only slight in nature, or they could require a major mental overhaul in attitude. But either way, most of us take the easy route and shy away but making any attempt at modifying our lives.

What is it that holds us back and keeps us from making necessary changes?

Denial plays a big role. It really is okay to admit that we have limitations, that we have made mistakes, that we have experienced moments of weakness, that we have found ourselves powerless in face of certain challenges. The point is there is no significant way to jump-start a future until we quit reflecting on the negatives of the past.

One of my all-time favorite stories is about Charlie Ward. His story fully illustrates the consequences of choices and the ability to jump-start a new future.

Charlie Ward's young-adult years in the early 1900s were spent in the Alaskan territory and Mexico, where he was part of Poncho Villa's army. Charlie was a thief and a gambler and ran narcotics. He was simply an all-around bad character. He was arrested, tried and convicted, and sent to Leavenworth Federal Penitentiary to serve a ten-year sentence.

Disillusioned with the way the first thirty-four years of his life had turned out, Charlie began to make changes in his attitude and thought patterns. He resolved to create a new Charlie and dispense of his wrongful ways of the past. While serving his time, he began to study and learn. His goal was to prepare himself for a better life after prison.

While he was there he met another man, Herbert Bigelow, who had been the president of the Brown & Bigelow company. He had been sentenced to Leavenworth for tax evasion. Bigelow had simply ignored a new tax law and was sent to prison as a result. Charlie Ward befriended Bigelow and helped him adjust to prison life. Mr. Bigelow was released before Charlie, but he promised Charlie a job when his incarceration was up. When Charlie was released, he went to work as a laborer for Brown & Bigelow.

Charlie wanted to advance in the company, which manufactured calendars and other promotional material, and advance he did. He learned the business inside and out and received greater opportunities and more responsibilities as time went on. He rose to vice president of the company under Mr. Bigelow. Upon Mr. Bigelow's unexpected death, he assumed the presidency. He served in that capacity for years and was held in high esteem in the business community. One of Charlie Ward's greatest contributions was the employment of former prisoners. In his tenure, Brown & Bigelow successfully employed hundreds of ex-inmates.

In 1935 President Franklin Roosevelt granted Ward a pardon to restore his civil rights.

It is worth noting that in the late 1940s Brown & Bigelow made calendars that featured a young blonde named Norma Jean. She later became famous under the name of Marilyn Monroe.

There may not be many Charlie Ward–type stories out there. But it does illustrate the point that we do have a choice in life. U-turns are allowed. At any point in our lives, we can make a decision to seek something better. We can choose to move beyond what has been for a greater reward in the future.

LETTING GO

I love the mountains of East Tennessee. Gatlinburg is one of my favorite places to visit. Not far from Gatlinburg, buried deep within a mountainside, is a cave with a lake called the Lost Sea. No natural light illuminates the lake, only man-made light.

For centuries, the lake was in complete darkness. But there is life inside the cave: the lake is inhabited by trout. No one knows how they got there, but the lake is full of them. These trout are different in two ways: First, they have no pigmentation. Their bodies are devoid of color since they have never been in sunlight. Secondly, the trout are blind. They have lived in total darkness all these centuries, so they have had no need for eyes.

Is there a lesson for us here? I think sometimes we are blind even with our eyes open. As Helen Keller once said, "The only thing worse than being blind is having sight and no vision."

Until we establish a vision of what changes we need to make, it will be difficult to make measurable progress going forward. The words of an unknown poet come to mind when I think of the inability to see that something different is needed in our lives: *Open your eyes that you may see the wonders of life that await thee.*

Have you opened your eyes to exploring alterations that will lead to a better life? I have no doubt that you want to be good, really good, in all areas of your life. I would also venture to say that you have already been successful at many aspects of living. But maybe you have slipped a bit here and there and want to return to your standard level of personal or professional excellence, a level where you felt happy and secure. Or maybe you are one who is reaching out for the first time toward the pinnacle of success. Am I hitting close to home?

No one knows this better than I do, but in life not everything always goes according to plan. There will be problems with finances, with marriages, with kids, at work, with personal issues . . . problems, period.

An old Spanish Proverb reads, "I don't want the cheese, I just want to get out of the trap." Is there some kind of trap that is keeping you from revolutionizing your life? To get out of a trap, slow down and determine the repair, maintenance, and tune-up that you must make to move to another level. You may find that some things you have done well in the past simply need a little tweaking here and there to jump-start your future again.

Many people who have made significant strides in their lives and their careers wrestled earnestly at the beginning with the challenge of how to jump-start the future. They somehow found the answer to let go and seek a better way to go. You can, too.

OLD WAYS

A clear fact when the intent is to jump-start your future is that you never let go completely of the old ways you have done things. Something of the past will always be left within you. Every new beginning carries with it a lesson from things you have done previously in your life

A variation in behavior that challenges a core belief, or is incompatible with how you have been doing things, is not always easy to pull off. Letting go is never easy. Altering the way you have done things requires the highest level of mental acumen and mental toughness.

Rock & Roll Hall of Famer John Cougar Mellencamp sang many hit songs. My favorite is "Hurts So Good." A couple of lines in that song are indicative of people who choose not to do something that could be in their own best interest: "Come on, baby, make it hurt so good / Sometimes love don't feel like it should . . . "

Are you one of those who doesn't want to give up something even when you realize it "don't feel like it should"? You are not alone. All around you are those who realize some of the things they are doing affect their quality of life, but they tend to ignore them because it "hurts so good."

If it hurts, even if it has been "good," why do people continue to do it? My observation is that people dislike the unknown that exists with change. Routine gives us a sense of comfort. If you couple that with many of the beliefs we have that are practically etched in stone, then you have a double-edged sword for leaving things just as they are.

Take those with serious health issues. Even a life-threatening health issue often does little to initiate appropriate life adjustments. Many with failing health find it difficult to make a life-enhancing transformation even when they know it will make their lives better.

"Hey, my health has been okay in the past; why will it not be okay in the future?" This is what a friend of mine once expressed to me after he found out he had lung cancer. He said this while smoking a cigarette. The capacity to make a change that might have a significant bearing on his health and life was not great enough to overcome the old ways. He is no longer with us.

Regardless of how short or long our "things to change" list is, most of us are very inflexible. We dislike contradictory factors that challenge long-felt beliefs. Even an Act of Congress would not cause many of us to make what could be beneficial changes. We prefer to live clutched to our old trappings. We forego something better at the expense of continuing along the same old comfortable path.

It is easier for us to discard responsibility for life-enhancing amendments than it is to accept them. Regardless of the adjustments that are needed, most of us say, *I'm doing okay with the way things are; why change now?* But familiarity is a battle cry that leads to mediocrity—or worse.

Let me ask you a straight-up question: Are those old ways still producing the quality of life you want? Or is it time to let go so you can create room for something better? You must learn to detach yourself from those things that feel "fine," to achieve greater things. You will not begin to initiate the desired conversion in your life until you do.

How we approach the process of changing our old ways makes all the difference in whether we do it successfully or not. What I am talking about is creating a mind-set in which things get better because we had the fortitude to do something to make them better. This is the mind-set that leads us to be deeply committed to jump-starting a better future.

Do you believe there is something better out there than you have ever experienced? If the answer is yes, then you have to do something different, and you have to do it deliberately. It works best when you have the ability to be proactive from insight that enables you to be reactive to needed adjustments. Armed with this kind of foresight, you can develop an arsenal of diverse strategies and tactics that will help you unlock the door to future success.

The key is to take something from the old ways, adjust your attitude to the present, and figure out a new take that will jump-start your future. Always work around the theory that your strength lies in the present. You live in the present. You work in the present. Therefore, take the present, make adjustments, and go on to what's next. This will differentiate and accommodate the kind of environment that will be favorable to enhancing the dash.

Life-Enhancement Message

Unless you are willing to leave some of your old points of view behind, you will seldom find yourself in a position to create something better—and possibly more lucrative—in the days ahead.

BUT NOW

How big is the gap between where you are now and where you would like to be? Can you put your finger on it?

But now are two simple words that indicate something must change if we desire to close that gap. Their meaning carries with it a huge responsibility of constantly seeking new avenues for a better life.

One of my "careers" was short-lived. For four years, I was a stockbroker with Merrill Lynch, Pierce, Fenner & Smith (just Merrill Lynch today), in Dallas. For the most part, my first six months were spent out of the office making calls on potential clients. At that time, the stock market was not very good. It was in the throes of what is known as a bear market.

However, I really enjoyed getting out and meeting people, and did so well at cold-calling that I received a certificate of recognition from the company. One of the individuals I met during my cold-calling was a gentleman by the name of Mel Ash.

Mr. Ash had his office in the same building as Merrill Lynch. Mr. Ash's wife was a lady known as Mary Kay. That's right, she was the founder of Mary Kay Cosmetics.

Mary Kay Ash epitomized how someone can take advantage of a "but now" moment. It occurred for her in the early 1960s, when she retired from a successful career in direct sales to pursue other interests. One of her other interests was to write a book for businesswomen showing them how to survive in the male-dominated business world. Her book contained two very distinct points. First, she wrote about what companies had done right for women, and then she wrote about how they could have done better. Upon completion of the book, Mary Kay realized she had inadvertently created a tremendous marketing plan for a company. It turned out to be a plan for her dream company, one that would provide women with the open-ended potential to achieve personal and financial success.

With her life savings of $5,000 and the help of her twenty-year-old son, Richard Rogers, Mary Kay launched Mary Kay Cosmetics on Friday, the thirteenth day of September in 1963. Later, with the financial assistance of Mr. Ash, Mary Kay Cosmetics rocketed to become one of the leaders in the industry. Over the next thirty plus years, Mary Kay's illustrious career earned her recognition as one of the top one hundred women of the twentieth century.

On a personal note, I was not very good at the stockbroking business. But one of the things I learned about myself in my abbreviated time with the brokerage firm was my effectiveness in speaking to groups of people. The financial seminars I presented in and around Dallas led to my "but now" moment.

During the next twenty-nine years, I spoke to over four thousand different groups (mostly sales groups). One of the main points in my presentation on sales was something I had learned from Mary Kay. It is the MMFI principle: **make me feel important**. It is the principle that is written in invisible ink on the forehead of every potential customer.

The Mary Kay story chronicles how a "but now" mind-set is crucial if one is to move beyond what is for the greater potential of what lies ahead. That's the direction you are headed, isn't it?

NECESSITY: MOTHER OF CHANGE

At this stage, we have developed the level of consciousness to let go and commit to jump-starting a new future. Change is in order, even as difficult as it may be.

Necessity has been called the mother of invention. It can also be called the mother of change. The capacity to change and adapt is what allows us to move forward. One of the most consistent things we can count on is that things around us are always undergoing transformation.

The theme of what you have read thus far in this chapter is that in order to keep up, we must actively seek out beneficial adjustments in our routines on a regular basis. We must set aside the old when the old can no longer guarantee fulfillment and provide for development.

Certainly not all modifications lead to growth, but there is no growth without making changes, for growth is never fixed or static. It is an ongoing event of awakening, development, adjustment, and adaptation.

I had a friend once tell me, "Most of us change, not because we see the light, but because we feel the heat." Whatever the motivation, just a simple change can get us moving in a more productive direction. It can sufficiently jump-start your future.

Is it time for you to say, "That's it. I'm done with the old way. I'm ready to turn over a new leaf. I'm ready to face the unpredictable and open myself to exploring new avenues. I can't wait. I'm ready to jump-start my future!"?

CHANGE IS PERSONAL

The fundamental nature of human beings is that making any kind of change is a personal issue. *Give me some facts and evidence that I can digest; then I will decide if it is in my best interest.* I guarantee that this is the attitude of most who read this book.

If I have made one thing perfectly clear in this chapter, it is that changing our mind-set about anything is very difficult to do—and virtually impossible for some people. Many are unlikely to adjust their position or opinion regardless of any evidence to the contrary.

Since change is one of the toughest mental challenges you will face in life, jump-starting your future and moving on to what may be something better take a lot of determination. Statistics from substantial research show that only one in seven will make meaningful alterations in the way they live life. We are what we are—creatures of habit—but habits can be changed. I am excited that, by virtue of reading this book, you are looking to transform your life.

I want to share with you a story about a former teammate of mine in the St. Louis Cardinals organization, who went on to a distinguished major league career. We will refer to him as Eduardo.

Eduardo had a difficult time with his teammates early in his career. He rarely spoke to any of them, and when he did it was to point out a mistake or to be critical of the play of a teammate. Like most players in the minor leagues of baseball, he was not only competing against an opponent, but he was also competing against his teammates.

The simple reason for his competition was that in the early 1960s there were approximately 650 players on major league teams' rosters, while there were several thousand competing at the minor league level, from Class D to Class AAA. In short, he was in competition for a place on a major league roster. To add to the pressure for a spot in the major leagues, the competition among minor league pitchers was even keener than among position players. The eight or nine pitchers on each minor league team were teammates competing against each other.

As a result of the pressure, Eduardo developed an attitude that made him extremely disliked in the clubhouse. His hostile feelings had an adverse effect on other players, thwarting his personal progress as a player. The repercussions of his poor attitude surfaced midway through the schedule the first year Eduardo and I were teammates.

It was late one evening when I heard a knock on my hotel room door. When I opened it I found Eduardo standing there with a black eye and numerous bruises on his face. He had been in a fight with another player he had been critical of earlier during a game.

Eduardo wanted to talk. Over two hours, and with many tears, I heard Eduardo's story. He had grown up with heavy criticism from his father, who had been critical not only of his performance but of other players, as well. Eduardo's dad also told him that his teammates were his enemies. "They want what you want, so don't be buddy-buddy with anyone."

I said very little to Eduardo, I mostly listened, but I did tell him one thing: "Eduardo, as elementary as this sounds, no one is perfect. We all are going to make mistakes playing ball and in life. Your teammates are not your enemies. Helping the team helps you get what you want. Until you get a grasp on that fact, you are going to have a hard time utilizing your great talent as a ballplayer."

"You think I can be good?" Eduardo asked with a quizzical look on his face.

"You can be as good as you want to be, but you have to get a handle on yourself," I offered with emphasis.

There was a slow transformation in Eduardo that season. Two years later we were teammates again. The critical nature that had marred his earlier baseball career was gone. He had stepped up to home plate and hit the ball out of the park.

Eduardo proved that the most important thing to remember about change is that it is an internal thing. I think the root of all personal alteration and the catalyst to actually begin creating life-changes is simple. It begins with the personal motivation of desiring the benefits of the change more than desiring the continuation of the status quo. This is the driving force that will allow you to start implementing a game plan that will jump-start your future.

The adventurous nature of this type of consciousness is the desire to move headstrong into making life-changing adjustments. It can carry you beyond the adverse attitudes and feelings associated with doing the same old things in the same old ways and expecting different results.

You begin to visualize future behavioral variations that will bring an improvement to what you have done in the past. You establish a foothold for what will move you to the next level instead of a continuation on the same path.

REDIRECTION

Now that you are ready to redirect your life and jump-start your future, the first phase of experiencing something different is a commitment to doing something different. The energy to pursue transformation with vigor and excitement lies within the consciousness of envisioning how the transformation will ultimately enrich your life. You must be very deliberate at looking at your current state of affairs and determining what's not working as well as you like—or once was—and what redirection you need to make.

The second phase is to develop a comprehensive strategy that lays out clear objectives for your life's mission going forward. If your present behavior or actions are not generating the kind of success and happiness you desire, then the focus is on putting them behind you and concentrating on what variations you need to jump-start your future.

The redirection questions before you then are these: What are you willing to do differently? Are you willing to step out of your comfort zone and expand your horizons? Are you ready to explore new territory and venture into the unknown, something that has not been a part of your regular daily routine?

The type and size of the redirection you wish to make are based on your personal choices. The consequences of your choices will do one of two things: either they will help clarify your commitments toward what you have been doing or they will lead you to make decisions that will allow you to more effectively jump-start your future.

The final phase in your desire to jump-start your future is the action phase. The difference-maker is to make sure that, through your redirection, you are headed in the right direction. Redirection is only a plus if it is in the right direction. You may not always know for sure, but if you've done your homework, you know in what direction you want to go.

DO IT NOW

Most alterations in your life will delve into the unknown. Consequently, you are probably not going to feel comfortable with them at first. This requires possessing a superior mental posture that accents a "do it now" *attitude*.

A favorite line I used when training salespeople was, "You gotta have a great starter, superb drivetrain, and weak brakes to be a great salesperson."

Getting anywhere, regardless of where it is, begins with how we start. We may possess tremendous attributes for our chosen endeavor, but they will be compromised and of little use without being a great self-starter. Whatever it is we need to be doing to improve, we can start anytime and anywhere, but we have to take the first step. But taking that first step sometimes is the toughest. Ty Boyd wrote, "Once you take that first step, you are almost 50 percent there."

That reminds me of a friend who wanted to undertake a new exercise program. He wrestled with the thought for several days. When I asked him if he had gotten started with his new adventure, his reply was classic: "I got it started today—I drove by the workout location in my car." My friend never started that regular exercise program.

It is amazing how those who are always talking about doing something tomorrow probably did the same thing yesterday. Too many of us have a tendency to put off until tomorrow what we need to be doing today to start building a better future.

What we do is succumb to one of the best salespeople around. His name is Procrastination. If there was ever a master at promoting deceit, it is this old pro. By the sheer genius of suggestion, he can make us believe all the negative reasons why a worthwhile change won't work. Believe me, this glib-tongued devil can turn an opportunity into no opportunity quicker than a wink.

There is no magic formula for overcoming the tendency to procrastinate, but we can start by being consciously aware of the importance of a do-it-now attitude. Here's a question that puts the right accent on the importance of having a do-it-now attitude: When you come eyeball-to-eyeball with tomorrow, are you going to wish you had done what you are not doing today?

Hit that starter and get moving. You can muster the courage to do it, even if that movement is foreign to you. I can sense that you are primed, even in a world full of distractions, to take that first step toward transformation. *I'll get started today.* That's the spirit!

NIX THE QUICK FIX

If we find ourselves behind the eight ball and need to quickly amend a life pattern, isn't there a tendency to go searching for a quick and easy fix? While it's important for us to adapt to evolving conditions, a quick fix, regardless of how innovative it may be, rarely makes for a significant improvement in any segment of life. The problem created by a quick fix is the lack of a solid base. Whatever adjustments we are hopeful of making should be built on the fundamentals that apply to that segment of our lives.

It's a lifestyle transformation, not something that is done for the moment to give the impression that we did something different. It must be a deliberate, thoroughly thought-out plan for it to be meaningful.

Babe Ruth, the great New York Yankee home run hitter, was once asked, "What are the fundamentals of hitting [a baseball]?"

Ruth's answer was, "See ball, hit the ball."

Ruth's rudimentary answer was fundamentally right. But there is probably nothing harder to do in sports than to hit a baseball. A batter has a hundredth of a second to make a decision before swinging, depending on what type of pitch is coming toward the plate and where is it located. No wonder a batter who gets three hits out of every ten official times at bat is classified as successful.

Digging for the fundamentals that apply to our search for new and innovative modifications is essential. While the challenges we face may not be as difficult as a baseball hitter's, they certainly are just important. You are not looking for a quick fix, you are looking for alterations that have staying power. Place your highest priority on effort and commitment, and the change will be as painless as possible. Focusing on the basics will make change more achievable and you more successful.

LEARN TO SAY NO

Achieving quality life adjustments, as we have seen, often means we may have to give up something to establish a path toward better results. Learning how to say no to ourselves is often the beginning of replacing old behavior with more positive behavior.

How good are you at saying no to yourself? Saying no to some old habits is often the crucial step in kick-starting the yeses in your life. There is real value in learning to say no to those activities that could take you away from performance-changing actions.

The key to saying no is to learn to be a "self-boss," for the more we "boss" ourselves from within, the less we will need to be bossed from without. In a very real way, we have to manage ourselves, or the time will come when we have nothing else to manage.

Would you consider yourself a self-boss? When you are a self-boss, something truly amazing takes place: you acquire the discipline necessary to replace the old you with the new you.

By saying no to unproductive or outdated activities, you are often saying yes to a brighter future. So learn the value of saying no to self-defeating strategies and activities.

Saying no is also very important in regard to your family. In your efforts to change and reach beyond to take on what you aspire to be, never neglect your family responsibilities. I have younger friends who still work 350 days a year, twelve to fifteen hours per day. In the process they make more money than they can ever spend, while ignoring their family and neglecting their health. Why?

Everybody can see their material success, but behind it are the ashes created by the chasing of false dreams. *I'm doing it for my family's future*, is the war cry.

Eventually, the truth is there for all to see when the family doesn't work out the way one wants. I was lucky. I was not a great dad, but thanks in great part to the mother of our two sons, things turned out well for them.

Let me share a story with you about a dad who wasn't as fortunate as me. We will call him Dick Hancock.

Dick is a highly successful businessman, the principal owner of a big steel-producing plant. I met Dick about twenty-five years ago under some very adverse circumstances.

It was on a Saturday afternoon in April. I would spend several hours on Saturday afternoon once a month at the church I was attending, talking with anyone who needed a willing ear and a caring heart. Dick's knock on the door that day was barely audible. When I opened the door I saw a man with pain stretched across his face that I could sense had arisen from his very soul. His body was slumped; tears flowed down his cheeks. His eyes were blood red.

It didn't take long to understand why Dick was there. He spoke hesitantly and painfully as he told me that his son had committed suicide the week before. He talked about how he had neglected his family while chasing his professional and financial goals. The sound of regret shook his voice as he told me his story. The suicide note that his son left said it all: *I had a father, but I didn't have a dad!*

I didn't try to give Dick any advice, I just listened, but I do remember telling Dick that he was going to have to be willing to live differently, not for his benefit but for that of his other son.

I later found out Dick did change. He became a dad to his other son.

Those of you who still have children at home, how many weekends in a year do you devote solely to your family? From the time a child is born until the time that child leaves home around eighteen, there are less than a thousand weekends available for you to be a parent. Think about that.

We don't have to tell our children how to live. Our purpose should be to live the way we want them to live and to let them watch us do it. Harmon Killebrew, a Hall of Fame baseball player, told this story about his childhood days: "My father used to play with my brother and me in the yard. One day Mother can out and said, 'You're tearing up the grass,' to which Dad replied, 'We're not raising grass, we're raising boys.'"

A true measure of how you are doing as a parent is summed up in this story.

"A worthy parent is one whose children run into their arms when their hands are empty." This unknown author had it right.

The final message here is simple: learn to say no to get to the yeses in your life.

SEVEN

THE ART OF BECOMING

Numerous years ago, a noted cartoonist for the Disney Corporation took time from his busy schedule, drawing the frames for a new movie to be called *Hercules*, to draw a caricature of me pitching a baseball. It became one of my most cherished possessions.

As a fan of caricatures, I have collected many over the years. One caricature in particular that stood out to me depicts a bum sitting on a park bench watching a chauffeured limousine ease by. The caption read, "Except for me, there goes I."

The reason those words mean so much is that they are so true. They point the finger in the right direction. If we fail to fulfill our dreams and aspirations in life, whom can we blame? If we are remiss in reaching our goals, whose fault will that be?

Can we blame our failures on circumstances? Who creates the major circumstances in which we find ourselves? Who ultimately makes the choices that alter who we are and where we are going? Can we place the blame on others? Can we honestly believe that other people have more influence on our decisions than we do? Or is the barrier to becoming the person we want to be, or to living the life we want, the person who looks back at us in a mirror? We are the chief architects of how life turns out for us, would you not agree?

Although our environment does play a role in achieving success, we do not have to be at the mercy of those circumstances. On the contrary, we can deliberately choose how those events affect our lives. We should never lay the blame for our lack of progress solely on the conditions around us. Regardless of external influences, we hold the power to make the best of anything we are confronted with.

Those who have gone on to greater heights have had to overcome some self-doubts about themselves. At times, they may have wondered if they were capable of meeting all the new challenges they would face as they traveled along life's road. But during these times of hesitation, they took stock of themselves. They believed they had the right stuff to make it big in the world of opportunity, and in spite of setbacks or feelings of doubt, their positive mind-set would propel them toward greater things. It was their mental fortitude that assured them that everything they needed was within themselves, and they never lost sight of that, even when the going got rough.

What are the options for a deaf-blind person to make it big in the world of opportunity? Helen Keller did. Her remarkable life story started in 1880. Helen was a healthy, growing child until the age of nineteen months. Then, as a result of an unknown illness, perhaps rubella or scarlet fever, Helen became deaf and blind. Beginning in 1887, against overwhelming odds, Keller's teacher, Anne Sullivan, helped her make tremendous progress with her ability to read and communicate.

Helen went on to college, graduating in 1904 cum laude from Radcliffe College. She was the first deaf-blind person to earn a bachelor of arts degree. A woman of superb intelligence and high ambition, Helen Keller was a crusader for the handicapped. She was a vocal advocate for people with disabilities. She cofounded the organization that later became Helen Keller International, an organization that supports veterans blinded in combat. Over time, its mission expanded to include combatting the causes and consequences of blindness, poor health, and malnutrition.

Keller authored numerous books. Her first book, *The Story of My Life*, is still in print in over fifty languages. During her outstanding life, Keller stood as a powerful example of how determination, hard work, and imagination can allow an individual to triumph over hardships. Helen overcame adverse conditions with a great deal of persistence and resolve, and grew into a respected and world-renowned activist who devoted her life to helping others.

Helen Keller's story illustrates that the barrier to achieving goals and satisfying dreams has very little to do with our physical capabilities. The greater indicator of becoming the person we are capable of becoming is the mental limit we place on the talents and resources we have at our disposal. It is the "why" and "how" in our heads, not the talents and abilities in our bodies, that ultimately determine our success. Although it may be cliché, "If there's a will, there's a way" *holds true when moving beyond the familiar and comfortable routine to reach beyond for something greater that enriches our lives and keep us evolving.*

Do you remember the ending to the movie, *The Wizard of Oz*? Dorothy says she doesn't have to look any farther than her own backyard to realize she has everything she needs to satisfy her heart's desire. Neither do we.

Life-Enhancement Message

That big adjustment you have been wanting to make in your life—do it now. Get a running start at it and jump right on in. You might just be surprised where you land.

EMBRACE WHO YOU ARE

Accepting who we are is the starting point for improving what we are. If we embrace who we are first, we have then positioned ourselves to visualize the person we can ultimately become. If we continually focus on our present state only, there will be little change. On the other hand, if we routinely envision the person we want to become and the direction we wish to go in life, it will be only a matter of time until our efforts carry us there. The law of attraction is a very powerful force.

I want to share a marvelous story about one of the most inspiring individuals I have ever met. His name is Jim Fowler. Jim's story promotes the role self-acceptance plays in making strides from who we are to who we can evolve into being.

The story begins on a cold, snowy day in February when I arrived at Logan Airport in Boston. I was there to do a marketing presentation to a large automotive group. When I arrived at the location for the event, Jim Fowler, the company's general manager, was there to greet me. As he welcomed me with a high level of enthusiasm, Jim did something unusual: he extended his left hand for the handshake. My first thought was that he had heard I was left-handed, and that was the reason for the left-handed handshake. But it only took a few seconds for me to understand why Jim was using his left hand. Jim didn't have a right arm.

Wanting to know his story, I asked if we could go to his office to visit before the main event started. Jim agreed. As we made our way there, I couldn't help but notice that he also walked with a slight limp.

After reaching his office and making ourselves comfortable, we sat down and Jim told me his story. He had been in Vietnam and lost both his right arm and right leg when he stepped on a land mine. Although the doctors told Jim he was lucky to be alive, he didn't agree. He thought, *What kind of life will that be for me?*

Feelings of sorrow and self-pity filled his days as he lay in the hospital bed during the months that followed. Jim spent very little time socializing, except with a young single amputee named Wilson McGregor. It was Wilson who would eventually play a key role in changing Jim's attitude—and his life.

When Jim was told that he would be able to receive an artificial leg but no arm, he was shocked. The doctors explained that they could not attach an arm to his badly mangled shoulder. That news drove Jim into an even deeper depression. Realizing how difficult it would be to learn to walk on an artificial leg without the balance afforded by an arm on that side of the body took all of Jim's hope away.

Consequently, he virtually refused to cooperate with the doctors and nurses, and his progress was slow. But then Wilson McGregor came into the picture. It was a statement from Wilson that spurred a change in Jim's attitude. Prior to leaving the rehab center, Wilson stopped by Jim's room to say goodbye. While there, Wilson emphatically offered Jim this advice: "Jim Fowler, you can lay around feeling sorry for yourself and do little or nothing with your life. But you have what it takes to walk out of here and enjoy a good life."

Fifteen years later I was sitting with Jim in his office listening to his story. Over that period of time, he had experienced immense success. It was quite evident that he had taken Wilson's words to heart.

I asked Jim what he thought Wilson meant by his comment "You have what it takes." He did not hesitate before answering: "I realized I still had the three things that are the most important to a human being. I had my head to think with and my heart to feel with, but most importantly, I had my guts to get me started and keep me going."

Jim Fowler exemplifies what we can accomplish when we realize we have what it takes to tackle life with all the gusto at our deposal, regardless of the difficulties we face. Jim also demonstrated what can happen when we focus on our strengths rather than our limitations, on the reasons why we can succeed and on what happens when we embrace who we truly are.

"If you are still living, you need to still be improving," is Zig Ziglar's reminder to us. Regardless of where we are on the ladder of success, it is wise for us to remember: everyone can make improvement in something that they do, even if it is in small increments.

KEY TO A WELL-LIVED LIFE

"We have met our toughest opponent, and it us."—Woody Hayes

The unfortunate truth is that our toughest opponent is one we are with 24/7. It is the one opponent that we must conquer to enjoy any measure of success and happiness in life.

A couple of personal questions arise about this opponent: Do you tend to sell yourself short and put limits on what you are capable of doing? Do you find it difficult to appreciate all the wonderful talents and resources you possess?

All we need to be great is already inside of us. We must simply appreciate that we possess the potential for living a well-lived life and then initiate the steps that lead us there. According to an old legend, when God was searching for a place to put the secret of a well-lived life, he decided to call his top angels together to discuss the situation. The angels soon met with God in a council meeting. When God asked for suggestions about where to put the secret of a well-lived life, one angel spoke up and said, "We should bury the secret deep in the earth."

"Not sure that will work," said God. "Some individual will dig down into the earth and find it. And once found, the individual finding it will share it with only a few."

"Maybe it should be sunk into the deepest ocean," related another angel.

"I'm afraid that won't work either," said the Lord. "Someone will dive into the deepest waters, search out the ocean bed, find it, and again hoard it for himself or just a few."

Then a third angel offered a recommendation: "Let's take it to the top of the highest mountain and hide it there."

But again God replied, "That one won't work either, for mankind will eventually climb every high mountain on earth. Someone will most surely one day find it and keep it for himself."

Gabriel, the lead angel, then spoke up. "Lord, we do not know where to hide the secret of a well-lived life, for it seems there is no place on earth or in the sea that man will not eventually reach and find it."

God surveyed the concerned look on the faces of the angels, and then he said, "Here is what we will do with the secret of a well-lived life." All the angels moved forward to the edge of their seats, eagerly awaiting God's response.

"We will hide it deep down within each person, and those who look for and find it there will not hinder the opportunity for others to find it for themselves." All the angels nodded in agreement with God.

Ever since God made that decision, the legend concludes, human beings have been going all over the earth, climbing, digging, diving, exploring, searching for something that they already have buried deep within themselves.

We were put us on this earth to succeed in living, not to fail. But it has been left up to each of us to claim this birthright—to be the author of a well-lived life.

The fulfillment of a well-lived life depends on releasing more and more of the undiscovered potential locked within us. We only start to utilize our potential when we are open to making the most of it. Potential is something we have always possessed. The reality of it is that we either use it or we lose it. When we make the decision to reach down into our inner being and maximize our potential, we will find ourselves doing things we always dreamed of doing, things we may have never imagined we were capable of doing.

LOVE YOURSELF?

I have been chomping at the bit to get this question on the table: Do you love yourself? It took me a long time to understand this "love yourself" concept.

The second of the biblical Ten Commandments says, "Love thy neighbor as thyself." This commandment often has been misunderstood and misapplied. What is the implication in this commandment?

It is simply this: when we love ourselves, we do not need to be the center of the universe. Loving yourself shifts the focus from yourself to others. It frees us of the need to feel selfish. We realize that through the giving of ourselves we enrich our own souls while we nourish the souls of others. It is extremely difficult to reach forward until we believe in and live the "love yourself" approach.

One of the common causes of stress and loss of confidence is an acute lack of self-love on the deepest level. So much time and energy are spent on creating a credible exterior that we often forget about the interior. We are more concerned about what others think of us than about what we think of ourselves. The old fear of "they" rears its ugly head.

Can you honestly look in the mirror and love the person looking back at you? If you don't love the main character in your life's story, that story is not going to work out like it should, or the way you want it to.

The first thing you have to do is begin with a little soul-searching. Introspection takes a great deal of courage, more than you may think. Although the real purpose should be to find the good within ourselves, we often find the search painful because of the tendency to focus on our weaknesses rather than our strengths.

Being aware of our strengths allows us to build on them and make strides in our lives as we go forward. I realize as much as anyone how arduous it can be to change the perception we have of ourselves. But once we begin to focus on our strengths, we find ourselves moving in a more positive direction.

Once we see the eventual results of change as being vital to a better life, we begin the process of altering how we look at ourselves. We choose to focus on our positive traits in order to build on them. Rather than continuing along the same path, making the same decisions, getting the same results, and feeling the same old way about ourselves, this amended perception of ourselves leads us to seek a better way of life, and enjoy even greater fulfillment as we do.

The vastness of the future is unknown. What is known is that this unknown future is just waiting for you to tackle it with the very best you. The very best you holds the key to realizing your dreams, aspirations, and ambitions, and it starts with a deep, abiding love of yourself.

POSITIVE EXPERIENCES

Why is it that some individuals with only average ability consistently perform above average, while other individuals with exceptional ability regularly fall short on quality results?

A significant part of the answer to this question can found in a person's self-image and how that person views past experiences. Those individuals with strong, positive self-images tend to recall and act on positive memories. Those individuals with weak, negative self-images tend to dwell on negative experiences and evaluations. What we have heard and thought in the past eventually becomes a part of our belief systems. It then turns out to be the direction our thought pattern takes us time and again in future situations.

A negative image is often accompanied by the mistaken belief that one lacks what it takes to be a highly effective performer. As long as past experiences are viewed in a negative way, how can there be a positive outcome? If we spend time focusing on the bad, we only create more negativism.

It has been my experience that those individuals who go on to bigger and better things refrain from dwelling on the negatives of the past.

By sheer determination and willpower, they cast off negative thoughts and comments. They have learned to stay in the now moment.

Highly successful people realize performing well can never be regarded as incidental or accidental. Instead, it is a direct reflection of their ability to shed any negatives that might arise from the past and focus on the positive and what is possible. Drawing on the positive events in their lives has helped them to continually develop their capabilities. Those positive things don't have to be from lofty achievements or full of accolades. On the contrary, even reaching small goals can serve an enormous purpose. Any experience that creates growth should be appreciated. It all counts in speeding up the process of getting to the good part faster.

PERSONAL BRAND

What is a personal brand? A personal brand originates in the depths of our being as our purpose for living and is expressed in our relationships and actions. Highly successful people find their purpose, build a brand based on it, and boldly express themselves through that brand. A personal brand permits the world to see the true, authentic you.

The key to making a personal brand work is to allow others to know us on a personal level. It is about our skills and talents. It lets us share what is unique about who we are and what we do. It is based on what we stand for and what is important to us. It also lets those who connect with us better understand what we believe in and why we believe it, helping them bond with us on an intellectual and/or emotional level. A personal brand helps definitively and consistently define and communicate what we are all about. It's the essence of what we want to achieve or experience in the world as we go forward.

The development of an authentic personal brand focuses on three questions: What is your "what"? What is your "that"? What is your "why"?

You may have settled on the answers to these three questions long ago without consciously realizing it. But there are many around us who are still struggling with the answers or who never even thought about this type of question.

Steve Olsher was a guest on my radio show several times. Steve wrote a bestseller entitled *What Is Your What?* Steve defines our "what" as our entire being, from the top of our heads to the bottom of our feet. Our "whats" are the talents and abilities we bring to the table.

Next up is your "that." When you say, "I am good at that," or "I enjoy doing that," what do you mean?

Are you able to come up with solutions, thinking outside the box? Are you able to step out of your comfort zone and move beyond the status quo? Are you good at handling projects that call for technical precision? Are you able to see opportunity amid problems? Are you a gifted communicator whom people tend to migrate toward and follow? Are you a natural-born leader? The design of a personal brand is primarily built around the answers to these questions. Formulate a simple, short statement to let others know the essence of your "that."

Now comes the big question of "why." Our "why" is what keeps desire high and provides the inner drive to keep us going when conditions are tough.

After you have written down a statement that describes your "what" and your "that," write down ten "whys" that describe why you want to succeed. Think in terms of the four facets that factor into leading a successful life: body, brain, heart, and soul. Do you have a good "why" in each of these areas that highlights your "what" and primarily your "that"?

Take two people with the same goals. One becomes a rousing success, while the other experiences little success at all. Why? The answer in many cases is found in the "why." All things being equal, the person who enjoys a high level of success does so because that individual has more "why" to want to succeed than the person who has limited success. Your "what" and your "that" are important, but if you want to achieve something great, get crystal clear on your "why." Your "why" will give the world a really good feel for who you are. This is the basis for building a personal brand that will resonate with those you interact with and those you hope to interact with in the future.

Your brand will strengthen your outlook and your confidence in yourself. The key element is to understand that it all begins with the attitude you hold toward yourself. When you have confidence in yourself, others will also have confidence in you. You won't have to blow your own horn, others will do it for you, and the sound will travel a lot farther.

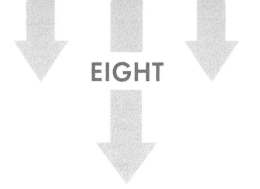

EIGHT

FOCUS ON THE POSITIVE

Things we did as youngsters can have a way of weathering the years and remaining in our minds as if they happened yesterday. One particular occurrence that has remained with me all these years occurred in a science experiment in elementary school. The basic ingredients used in this experiment were a jar filled with clear water, some mud, and a water faucet. The mud was placed in the jar of water and stirred enough to completely permeate it. The jar was then placed under a dripping faucet. Drop by drop, the muddy water began to clear. By day's end, the water in the jar was virtually clear. Only a small bit of muddy residue was visible.

Making positive changes in our lives occurs the same way. Muddy, negative attitudes respond to the gradual addition of doses of positive input until the major focus is on the positive.

There is no question in my mind that the attitudes we live by create the kind of world we live in. The only thing we can really control in life is our own mental attitude. So, to change anything, first we must change our attitude. When we possess the right kind of mental perspective and toughness to recognize and develop our potential, we move forward to becoming the successful person our vision tells us we can become. We tend to perform in the way that we have envisioned.

Approaching life with a positive, forward-looking attitude does not create new talents and abilities. It simply helps us recognize, appreciate, and utilize the talents and abilities we already have. It is important to remember that, as we saw in the previous chapter, talents and abilities are not something we simply possess, they are something we use. Even more important to remember is that the more we use them, the more we find available to use.

Life-Enhancement Message

We are our attitudes and our attitudes are us.

WALK ON THE SUNNY SIDE

There is an old song called, "On the Sunny Side of the Street." It is a sound testament to the importance of looking at life through rose-colored glasses. The simplicity of looking on the "sunny side" is that it demonstrates to others the joy of living that resides within each of us. It is not necessary for us to wear a sign telling people how we feel on the inside. They see it. They feel it. They see it in our actions and hear it in our voices. They sense it in our words and feel it in the energy around us. They recognize the incredible amount of joy that can flow from our lives when we are "walking on the sunny side of the street."

Every day we will have ample opportunities to show how looking on the sunny side can make a difference in our own life as well as in the lives of others. Those around us will be drawn to the optimistic passion and enthusiasm we exude on a consistent basis. They will desire to experience some of the excitement we possess. They will want some of the glow and warmth that we bring to our daily activities.

Those who know me well refrain from bringing up negative stuff when I am around. When someone starts speaking badly of someone or something, my response is simply, "Whoa. Hold on. I can't go there." I say it with a wink and a smile. I have received many blank stares and questions, like "You can't go where?" It is nothing personal.

It's just in my DNA. *Please, no negative energy in my space*—that's my take. What's yours?

Life-Enhancement Message

Pay close attention to your attitude because your attitude will determine the outcome of most things that occur in your life.

POSITIVE OUTCOMES

Do you believe in miracles? I do. I have personally witnessed three miracles that occurred in the lives of my family and friends. Two involved family members, while the third was in the life of the son of a business partner. Here are their stories.

My nephew, Clay Miller, had a tragic accident while driving an ATV in the summer of 2000, right before his senior year in high school. The ATV he was driving hit a small ditch and flipped forward. Clay had no helmet on, and when he slammed the ground with his head, he was critically injured.

The prognosis was not good. For thirty-one days, Clay was in a coma. But then, miraculously, on the thirty-first day, his eyes opened and he was once again awake and aware of the world around him.

Clay went through a laborious, painstaking recovery. During that period, I had the chance to push him in a wheelchair at the Spain Rehabilitation Center, in Birmingham, Alabama.

As I wheeled Clay on an elevated walkway that crossed over a major Birmingham street, he raised his head to look at the traffic flow. He appeared startled and stared at the traffic for a few seconds. I could tell by his reaction that something was going on in his brain. This incident gave me a glimmer of hope for Clay's recovery. I left the hospital that day a great deal more confident that Clay would be able to resume a normal life. But I also realized that Clay would have to relearn many things to reach that stage.

For example, Clay remembered that there were two men with him after the accident had occurred. They were telling him to hold on. But he didn't know who they were. However, after seeing pictures of his two late grandfathers, Buddy Vickery and Earl Miller Sr., Clay said, "Those are the men I remember." I really don't know the psychological significance of that. I only know that it played a role in Clay's fight to live.

Less than a year later, Clay returned to play baseball on a state championship team his senior year in high school. Today he leads a productive life.

The next story is of Jose Nunez, the seventeen-year-old son of a former business associate of mine. While fishing during a thunderstorm, Jose was struck by a bolt of lightning. Jose was in a coma for fifty-two days, barely hanging on to life. The doctors were pessimistic about his odds to live, and if he did survive, their prognosis was not promising.

The family, however, remained optimistic. They were looking for a positive outcome. They were looking for a miracle. However, with no progress being seen in his recovery, the family finally decided to unplug all life-support mechanisms. The night before this was to occur, Jose opened his eyes. He promptly said to his mother, who had been in that hospital room by his side for all fifty-two days, "Mom, I'm thirsty. Can I have a glass of water?"

Jose has experienced some mental challenges over the years, but twenty-two years ago, he started his own lawn-care business. This was about the same time he met a wonderful young lady named Caroline. Today, the husband-and-wife team of Jose and Caroline has a thriving business, one that employs over twenty people.

The third and final story is about my oldest sister, Priscilla Wilder. She is known as the "miracle lady." Priscilla's story epitomizes how having a positive mind-set can make a difference in living—period.

In 2004 Priscilla was involved in a most unusual and potentially deadly accident. It happened on a Saturday morning in October in Auburn, Alabama. Priscilla and her family were planning to attend a home football game for the Auburn University Tigers. Prior to leaving for the stadium, Priscilla wanted to make a quick trip to the grocery store to procure a few items for the tailgate party.

Getting into her SUV, Priscilla started the vehicle, engaged the gearshift, and put the car into reverse, but she could not disengage the parking brake because of the severely inclined driveway. As a result, she asked her son, Ty, to undo the parking brake while she exited the vehicle and walked behind it to notify the kids playing in the driveway that she was about to back up.

Just as Priscilla reached the back of the vehicle, Ty disengaged the parking brake. He didn't realize that his mother hadn't moved the gearshift into the park position. The vehicle immediately began to roll backward. The rapidly moving SUV knocked Priscilla to the ground and proceeded to run over her body as the family helplessly watched. Both rear and front wheels ran over Priscilla's body, crushing her chest cavity and smashing both lungs while severely bruising her liver and heart.

It took the ambulance almost twenty-five minutes to arrive because of the massive traffic caused by the football game crowd. How she lived even that long without lung capacity is amazing. By the time the ambulance arrived at the hospital and the emergency-room staff could assist, almost an hour had passed. Priscilla lay there conscious the whole time.

The doctors gave Priscilla about a 10 percent chance of living. The medical staff decided to place her traumatized body in a drug-induced coma that would last three weeks.

Our mother, Ruth, was by her bedside for seven weeks. Her husband, Billy, was there on a daily basis, as well. An interesting sidebar is that Billy slept on the floor during the hospital stay, and he still sleeps on the floor today.

With each passing day, the medical personnel and the family alike became more hopeful that Priscilla would survive, but with what kind of life? That was a question that circled around in our minds. Now, fourteen years later, Priscilla still experiences some discomfort, but she has been able to enjoy a very fruitful life. And, most importantly, her strength, courage, and positive outlook have offered hope to many.

I believe divine intervention is an important factor in "miracles." But I also believe the mind-set of those individuals personally involved in the miracles is significantly important, as well. A positive nature leads to a positive outcome. Study after study has shown that people with a positive, optimistic attitude live longer and healthier lives. They also have more energy, make better decisions, perform better, are more productive overall, and are less stressed. Finally, they are happier, have more quality relationships, and have more success in their careers than do pessimists.

However, there has been a lot of misunderstanding about what it means to create and maintain a positive mind-set. It takes a lot more than repeating a lot of feel-good one-liners (even though they help), to make positive thinking work in our lives. It takes discipline, commitment, and a proper understanding of what being positive and optimistic really means. Positive thinking holds us in good stead in a world that is constantly throwing difficult challenges at us. It allows us to mitigate the negative effect that even a tragic event or circumstance can have on our lives.

PLAYING TO WIN

Years ago, I was sitting in the office of Coach Bum Phillips the day after his heavy-underdog New Orleans Saints football team had upset the Los Angeles Rams. He was speaking with a sports reporter and said something I have never forgotten: "We were playing to win, while they were playing to keep from losing."

The more I thought about that statement, the more I realized how true it was. Several questions arise from Bum's quote that we should be asking ourselves: What kind of frame of mind do we possess when we approach a difficult task or a crucial situation? Do we focus on what can go right, or is our attention geared mostly to what might go wrong?

When our attention is centered on the things that we should be doing, the things that can go right, our actions will reflect this positive approach. The odds will be in our favor when we keep our eyes on what we should be doing to be successful.

Conversely, when we consistently think about what we shouldn't do rather than what we should do, where is the effort being placed? What are we actually focusing on? Aren't we intuitively tuning into the "don'ts" instead of the "dos"—the negatives instead of the positives?

To avoid a negative "keep from failing" attitude, we simply need to refrain from thinking about the negatives that can hold us back. When we place emphasis on that which is positive—that which makes up a success-oriented attitude—it will most likely direct our performances in a way that makes our intended outcome a reality.

Which is more indicative of you? Is this an area in your mind-set at which you need to take a serious look?

Occasionally, it is important to check your focus. Ask yourself questions like *Am I focusing on what I can do rather than what I cannot do? Am I focusing on what can go right rather than on what might go wrong? Am I focusing on what it takes to be successful, or am I focusing on what it takes to just keep from failing?*

Think on these words about having a positive attitude:

> The quality of your attitude determines your fate;
> Change is possible if needed—it's never too late;
> For it is true, the attitudes you choose to possess
> Will lead either to failure or overwhelming success!

ATTITUDE OF EXPECTANCY

Is the glass half full, or is the glass half empty? The answer to this age-old question says a lot about the way we look at life. When we create a mental picture of being successful, we are training the mind to expect and work at what it takes to be successful. In a very real way, we make success happen by getting into a pattern of believing success will happen. We become endowed with a special kind of attitude that creates conditions and actions that help us succeed.

Success is truly the product of a mind-set. If you have an internal set of expectations that you can accomplish something, those expectations alone will enhance your chances of realizing accomplishments. Good things are more apt to come your way when you are expecting them. When you possess the power of positive expectancy, watch your success ratio go up.

Now, believing you are going to be a champion may not make reaching that level any easier, but it does mentally increase the possibility. It not only improves your chances of achievement, it also makes the periods between important events a great deal more pleasant. You live in the exciting expectancy that your best performance is just around the corner.

We need to store this away in our mental computer: It is important to believe something is so before it becomes so, in order to be sure that it will be so.

Life-Enhancement Message

You can expect to succeed, or you can expect that you are going to fail. Either way, your prevailing attitude will contribute to making it a reality.

LANGUAGE OF SUCCESS

One of the first steps in focusing on the positives of life rests upon the simplest strategy, a strategy that if you stick with it, using it over and over, almost guarantees success. This simple strategy is to always speak the language to success to yourself.

Talking negatively to ourselves is a very common habit. We tend to be our toughest critic because we want to enhance what we are doing. We want to be more efficient and effective today than we were yesterday. But more often than not we are tougher on ourselves than conditions warrant.

Do you tend to be your toughest critic? Are you tougher on yourself than conditions may warrant? Do you try to "motivate" yourself by tearing yourself down rather than building yourself up?

When you talk yourself "down," you tend to focus on what you aren't doing or feel you can't do. As a result, you keep your faults and flaws front and center in your mind. You have focused on a negative you. In this desire to motivate yourself to perform better, you are actually tearing yourself down rather than building yourself up. Privately, you are saying to yourself, *I'm not good at this,*" or *I'm not good at that.* And the more you tell yourself you are not good at it, the more convinced you will become. Reality will, in kind, reflect this.

Now, you might say, *I really don't mean these things I am saying to myself about myself.* Seldom do we really "mean" them. But isn't there an inherent problem here?

Self-talk has a way of becoming a self-fulfilling prophecy. Each time we express a negative statement to ourselves, we take a step forward in getting good at being bad to ourselves. We put poison into our system without giving much thought to the consequences. When we focus on negative self-talk, and talk about what we aren't doing or can't do, how can anything positive occur?

SELF-TALK BASE

How we perform will always be consistent with what we think. And what we think is largely influenced by what we tell ourselves about our ability to perform and our confidence to achieve results. Without the support of our self-talk, it is extremely difficult to perform at a high level. Action on the outside consistently follows the action on the inside. We probably innately know this, but some of us continually underestimate the power our self-talk has on personal success. We must strive for accurate and realistic inner conversations.

It is from this base that we can challenge the erroneous assumptions and beliefs we have developed over time about ourselves. Then we are in a position to follow the route determined by the new and more accurate inner messages.

Is this a concern of yours? Do you have a tendency to talk negatively to yourself about yourself? I think you realize the importance of what your inner voice is saying. I believe you recognize that you cannot talk with yourself in negative terms and expect affirmative results. If it's something you need to work on, now is the time to begin.

MONITOR YOUR SELF-TALK

In this area of correcting self-talk we must muster as much mental muscle as humanly possible. It is crucial to making the most of our life-fulfilling opportunities. Though it takes a lot of focus and discipline to change old self-talk patterns and attitudes, it is possible to turn the unfamiliar into the familiar.

Changing our self-talk habits begins with monitoring our self-talk. We need to listen to ourselves, notably when we are facing a tense or stressful situation. Being aware of what we are saying to ourselves about ourselves is the beginning of the process of refining our self-talk. Once we take this first step, we will find ourselves making key adjustments to our self-talk patterns.

In this process, we are working toward two very different goals. First, learn what situations have a tendency to trigger negative comments. Ask yourself, *What am I telling myself about this particular situation that is negative and self-defeating?* Secondly, the goal is to effectively change your inner dialogue to fit a more positive and upbeat direction. A great tool to use here is the "take two" technique used in making movies. When you do slip up and talk negatively about yourself, simply back up and strike it from the record, and begin anew.

Fueled by the thrust of this positive approach, you begin to make strides in improving your self-talk and your performance. You may feel a bit strange or uncomfortable talking to yourself in a new way, but it gets easier and easier. As you do this, be aware that you will be giving the old programming in your subconscious mind quite a shock. It is not accustomed to the wonderful new descriptions you are using in describing yourself. But it can learn.

Any way you look at it, when you talk in a positive, upbeat way to yourself about yourself, everything else will have a way of taking care of itself. So here is my suggestion: For the next twenty-one days, consciously focus on speaking "up words." Tell yourself what is right with you, not what is wrong; what you can do, not what you can't do. What you want to happen, not what you don't want to happen. Dwell on your pluses, not your minuses. Use your enthusiasm and energy to lift yourself up, not to put yourself down. Remember, your self-talk has brought you to where you are, and it most surely will carry you where you want to go.

AIDS TO SPEAKING "UP WORDS"

- Keep a close tab on your "apostrophe tees." You know the ones I'm talking about: *can't, won't, shouldn't, wouldn't,* and *don't.* The more you use these in a personal sense, the more negative you become. Work to eliminate as many apostrophe tees from your self-talk as you possibly can.

- Don't tie yourself in "nots." If you persist in using self-defeating statements, they become a self-fulfilling prophecy. Eliminate the "nots," for the more you tell yourself that you are not good at doing something, the more convinced you become. Untie these "nots" in your self-talk:

> The can nots
> The do nots
> The will nots
> The may nots
> The could nots
> The would nots
> The should nots
> The am nots

Especially the "am nots." For example, *I am not good enough.* Sure you are!

- What-if. Do you say things like *If I was this, I would be better at that,* or *If I had that, I would be better at this*? What-if statements never make you better. In fact, they are success stoppers.

- Get off your "buts." There is no way you can keep up with the changes happening around you if "Yes, but . . ." becomes your hallmark. Listen to how many times you tell others all the reasons why you can or will do something and then, in the next breath, offer a "but" followed by all the reasons why you cannot. Amazing how everything before the *but* has little or no significance. So a wise decision is to *get off of your "buts."*

- Here is the positive step. Learn to use the "in the bag" concept. Whatever you want to change or improve, state it in the present tense as if it is an accomplished fact. Make self-talk statements like *I am, I have, I do.* When you use this kind of positive language long enough and persistently enough, it will eventually come to fruition. It becomes a part of your belief system.

I leave you with this bit of wisdom from an unknown source:

Keep your THOUGHTS positive
Because your thoughts become your ACTIONS.
Keep your ACTIONS positive
Because your actions become your HABITS.
Keep your HABITS positive
Because your HABITS become your WORKING STYLE.
Keep your WORKING STYLE positive
For your WORKING STYLE becomes your
SUCCESS FORMULA.

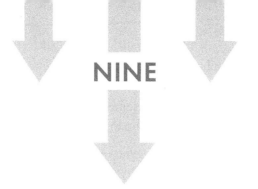

NINE

BUILDING SOCIAL CAPITAL

Developing and building social capital is extremely crucial in this age of electronic devices. But it appears to me that the fine art of finding, making, and keeping relationships has certainly taken a back seat in the social media era.

There is no doubt in my mind that social media has changed the playing field for interpersonal relationships. Building social capital calls for moving beyond the medium of electronic devices. Undoubtedly, some people are blessed with a greater receptivity for social interaction than are others. But because someone may have more personality doesn't mean others shouldn't develop their own personalities, does it?

I would be the first to admit that personality is a vague, intangible thing. It may be reasonably difficult to explain, but it is not so difficult to recognize, is it?

Can one improve their personality? Sure they can. Do I hear you asking, *What can I do specifically to develop my own? How can I improve my ability to get over the receptivity hurdle?*

First, you have to set a goal of interacting more with others. Your personality will grow the more you interact with other people. Secondly, it is crucial that you realize the importance of approachability. Just how approachable are you?

Better approachability might develop or even add a magnetic spark to your personality. It is a key factor in developing a more personable demeanor. Do you need some sprucing up in this area? Having the mental fortitude to measure up to the task is a great place to start.

Life-Enhancement Message

Don't judge others by their covering, casting them away as ugly or heavy or difficult. Beneath the covering, you will find something of splendor, woven of love, filled with wisdom, and full of life. The spirit of your task is to discover it.

—From the writings of Fra Giovanni (1519 AD)

APPROACHABILITY

In the people business, we can always count on being under the microscope. And that microscope has a way of pointing out any flaws in our person-to-person people skills. Experts say that, during the first couple of minutes of meeting someone for the first time, the tone is set for the ultimate and continuing success of the relationship. Right or wrong, fair or unfair, first impressions are vitally important.

Probably nothing is more important in getting a new relationship off the ground than the initial impression we make on someone. Our ability to make a favorable initial impression is dependent in large measure on our approachability. Approachability can best be described as a special appeal we possess that attracts others to us with ease and comfort.

In building social capital, it's important to spend quality time developing and honing our approachability skills. It is easy to overlook the importance of continually improving our ability to make an inspiring first impression. But a word of caution: Don't try too hard to make an effective first impression. Exerting too much effort to impress others, not too little, is what turns others off. The smart move is to consciously take the focus off of yourself and place it on the other person.

APPROACHABILITY INVENTORY

Let's get real specific. Here are some reminders of what it takes to have good approachability:

- **Be positive.** Your first priority in being more approachable is to be positive, direct, and specific in your initial approach. No hint of doubt about yourself or your appearance. No negative thoughts about what others might think of you, either.

- **Prepare your appearance.** Do you look and dress like someone who is ready, willing, and able to make a great first impression?

- **Display a happy face.** Do you put a happy face on regardless of your mood? Placing a smile on your face before meeting someone rounds out your wardrobe. You can smile your way into the hearts of others, but you will never frown your way in.

- **Create a safe environment.** Don't be afraid; enjoy your time with people. Make them feel as if you would rather be with them than anywhere else.

- **Make eye contact and give a firm handshake.** No further explanation is needed, except the reminder that this is generally your first action when you meet someone.

- **Call others by their names and do it often.** First time meeting, ask, "May I call you Mary (or John)?" Is there anything sweeter to the ear than to be called by your name? Every time you get a chance, call the person by name.

- **Speak and act enthusiastically.** Come on now, aren't you glad that others give you a piece of their prime time? Show your excitement for the opportunity in what you say and how you say it.

- **Be considerate of time.** Demonstrate to others that you will have their best interests at heart by maximizing the time you spend with them. Being cognizant of time leads to saying what you must say, not what you could say.

- **Be thoughtful of opinions, considerate of feelings.** Listen with an open mind to what others have to say, and try to gauge the feelings behind their words.

- **Create early involvement for others.** The information you provide to others is only as good as the information they want and need to hear. Find out what their interests may be, and move the conversation along those lines.

- **Be patient and courteous—don't rush.** What do you need to know? Others will tell you all about themselves if you will just take the time to ask and listen.

SOCIAL CAPITAL TOOLS

Let's turn our attention now to some of the tools we use in building social capital. These tools include listening, questioning, our tone of voice, the words we speak, humor, and smiling.

We begin with the importance of listening. Do you realize that we listen people into our way of thinking, we don't talk them into it? Are you aware that it is easier *not* to listen than it is to listen? Research shows that the average human hears at a rate of 400–600 words a minute and speaks at the rate of about 125–150 words a minute.

Even with this wide discrepancy between the ability to hear and the ability to speak, we probably understand only about 25 percent of what is being said. This is because we can listen faster than a speaker can speak. As a result, there is a tendency for us to mentally stray and begin to think about what we want to say in return.

LISTENING LEADS TO ACTION

Building social capital starts with our ears, not our mouth. As we improve the quality of our listening, we improve the quality of our impact on others. Obviously, our Maker was telling us something when he gave us two ears and only one mouth!

- The quality of listening plays an impactful role in building social capital in the following manner:

- We learn nothing about others by telling, but there is no limit to what we learn by asking and listening.

- The easiest route to making an impact on others is not the information we give to them but the information they give to us. We see a lot by listening.

- Through listening, we display a greater interest in others. This leads to them showing a greater interest in us and what we have to say.

- When we listen and observe, we do a much better job of gathering information that leads to better understanding.

- Listening helps us pick up clues to make sound and reasonable decisions in our relations with others.

- Listening reflectively helps us help others answer questions that might be circling in their minds.

- Listen wisely. Observe carefully. Consider thoughtfully. Respond appropriately.

LISTENING ATTITUDES

- **Limit your own talking.** You can't talk and listen at the same time. Listen with your whole being and "feel" the spoken words.

- **Listen for thought patterns, not just words.** It is important to listen to the point of view being expressed instead of reacting to how it's presented. The words are important, but the *thoughts* behind the words are more important.

- **Focus on what is being said.** As established earlier, listening speed is faster than speaking speed. As a result, it is easy to lose concentration. Consciously focus on the whole message, not the "bits and pieces."

- **Don't interrupt.** Hear the speaker out. Provide a "full hearing" for the speaker to express his or her thoughts and feelings. Then, when the speaker finishes talking, pause for a moment before you speak.

- **Don't jump to conclusions.** Be patient. Listen to everything with an open mind. Jumping to conclusions is not an exercise you undertake when in conversation mode.

- **Listen between the lines for emotions.** Eighty percent of what is being said is emotions. If you are only listening for facts, you are only receiving 20 percent of the entire message. Listen for feelings as well as facts.

- **Ask for details.** If the speaker tends to be too technical, or the subject of the message is unfamiliar to you, ask for greater details to help you understand. Then repeat it all back to be sure you are both in agreement before proceeding.

- **Use silence.** Silence is a great tool for controlling the flow of the conversation. Quality listening involves the use of pauses and moments of silence prior to your responses.

- **Restate what you think you heard.** Restate the opinions or points of view of the speaker. Focus on the key points. It is a way of saying, *Is this what you mean?* Ask for clarification. Don't assume. If the speaker makes a point that is unclear to you, say, "What I understand you are saying is this, is that right?"

- **Ask for feedback.** Show your desire to understand the speaker's message by asking for feedback or clarification: "You feel that you want _____, is that right?" "Do I hear you saying _____?"

REFLECTIVE LISTENING SKILLS

Relationships in our overprogrammed society are not easy to develop, nor to sustain. Enter reflective listening. Utilizing reflective listening skills is a rock-bottom prerequisite for maintaining a relationship over the long haul.

Is what we heard really what the person was trying to say? This is the crux of our mission.

Reflective listening skills involve two key steps: seeking to understand what the other person is saying, then restating what we heard to confirm our understanding. It is an attempt on our part to reconstruct what we believe someone is thinking and feeling, and then offering our reflective understanding.

Reflective listening is a specific strategy. It is intensely demanding. It involves listening with intent and effort. It should never be entered into with a careless or halfhearted attitude. It requires concreteness and relevance to be effective. There is a time and place in the incredibly complex realm of relationships where reflective listening will make a difference in the growth of our personal relationships.

Reflective listening applies at home, at work, at school. It is the centerpiece of the problem-solving process for those problems that involve those close to us. Sometimes all someone needs is a willing listener to clarify his or her own thinking. Our role may be to ask a few probing questions or to make a suggestion or two, but mostly it is to listen. More often than not, the solution for the person's problem will come from within; it was always there. We simply, through reflective listening, help the person find it.

Don't underestimate the importance of being a good listener. It is a sure way to gain influence and credibility and grow your social capital.

THE QUESTIONING TECHNIQUE

Another great social capital development tool is effectively using questions. We begin with "the questioning technique."

The best way to get to know people better is to ask questions. Your capacity to get others to listen to you is only as great as your capacity to listen to them. Think on these things:

- When you ask questions, display a sincere interest in learning all you can about others. It also helps them better understand their own reasoning behind what they have to say.

- Questions put you in a better position to find a common area for developing the communication process. You don't have to guess about what to talk about.

- Questions function as a way to understand perspective. Questions are windows to the minds of others. They inspire greater participation in the communication process.

- Treat all questions asked of you as compliments, for if they are important enough for someone to ask, they should be important enough for you to provide sufficient answers.

TYPES OF QUESTIONS

There are two main types of questions that we can ask: open-ended questions and closed-ended questions. Open-ended questions help us draw out and explore possibilities with others. Closed-ended questions are typically objective in nature and seek specific, factual information.

Open-ended questions start with one of the following seven words:

1. *Who* develops uniqueness.

2. *What* develops narratives.

3. *When* develops the time period.

4. *Which* develops a choice.

5. *Where* develops a place.

6. *Why* develops motives and details.

7. *How* develops explanations.

The use of the closed-ended questioning technique should involve three decisions:

1. What questions to ask.

2. How to phrase the questions.

3. When to ask the questions.

Examples of closed-ended questions are, How old are you? Where do you work?

TONE OF VOICE

Do you realize that every time we speak, we speak twice? I don't mean that we speak with a "forked tongue." What I mean is that the words that come out of our mouths convey our thoughts, while our tone of voice reflects our attitude. What we say is important, but the way it is said is even more important.

Think of your own experience. You sense when someone is telling you something but their tone of voice isn't backing up what they are saying. How often have you been on the other side of the equation, where your body language didn't quite measure up with your words?

Research has shown that as much as 90 percent of friction in our lives is caused by the mere tone of voice. Most of the time, in our conversations with others, the effect of tone is separated from the effect of the words spoken. Therein lies the rub. Unless the tone of voice and the words spoken are in accord, the communication process is compromised.

I hope you hear me saying that tone of voice is just as effective as words in communicating with others. There is little to gain and much to lose when the voice tone is out of line with the words used.

Keep reminding yourself that words serve little genuine purpose unless they are backed up by the tone of voice. When these two are in accord the ability to communicate is greatly enhanced.

Primarily voice tone is an expression of attitude. Disinterest, indifference, disagreement, resentment, and the like are chiefly the reasons for a negative tone of voice. These feelings may have a right to exist, but when our tone grinds with bitterness or even shows accents of attempted politeness, it does little to boost the message we are trying to get across.

When we are constantly aware of the importance of our tone of voice in the communication process, we can begin to discipline ourselves to deliberately adopt a more agreeable tone. The ability to get our points across or heal a brewing feud can be more effectively accomplished when our tone and our words are in accord.

Just think of the persuasive tone used to make up after an argument or when we wanted to obtain something from a difficult person. What did we do? We intently focused on ensuring that our tone of voice matched our words. It simply makes sense to incorporate these same qualities in our speech all the time.

WATCH YOUR WORDS

Have you ever given much thought to the fact that words have no meaning except the meaning given to them by people? Think about that for a minute. Words can add to life. They also can take away from life. The old rhyme "Sticks and stones may break my bones, but words will never hurt me" is far from the truth.

The kind of words that add to life have an endless echo. They seldom go in one ear and out the other. In fact, words that soak into our consciousness are spoken softly and gently, not loudly and harshly.

On the other side of the coin, words can leave lasting damage. We all know what it's like to be on the receiving end of verbal abuse. "When is the last time you did anything right?" "Which one are you, dumb or dumber?" These statements are examples of verbal abuse. And when someone adds the excuse "I'm just kidding" to the mix, the pain is even greater, isn't it?

Verbal abuse can happen in any relationship. Put-downs and insults can penetrate like a sword. They can leave emotional scars. They can do as much damage as any form of abuse. Verbal abuse arises from deep within and is based on a desire for control and possession of power. It shows the destructive nature of the inner person.

Are you on either side of the verbal abuse issue? Do you need help in breaking this vicious cycle? I am not qualified to go any farther than to say please get professional help. Those close to you deserve it, and your desire to have quality relationships depends on it.

Let's close this segment on words with a good dose of wisdom and a tad of wit:

- If we talk too fast, we often say something we haven't thought of—yet. So if we slow down and speak with tact, then we will have less to retract.

- We don't have to explain something that we didn't say, do we? I can assure you that among our most prized possessions are some words we have never spoken.

- Believe me, if we don't say anything about something we know little about, we won't say anything we wish later that we had not said. What's the saying—"Better one word before than two after"?

- There is absolutely no physical or scientific evidence that the tongue is attached to the brain. That makes a wise decision one in which the brain is turned on before putting the tongue in gear.

- One of the best ways to save face is to be careful how we use the lower part of it. Along those lines, I have learned that others don't mind what we have to say so long as we say it in a few words.

HUMOR

"Laughter is where we feel good all over but principally show it in one spot."—Josh Billings

Those who know me well will tell you that I love to laugh. I spent my early life being much too serious. Humor arrived in my life at about the right time. It is amazing how it sometimes takes a medical issue to change our lifestyle. Has that happened to you? It did to me. Maybe even today, I don't smell as many roses as I need to, but I can promise you I slow down for a good laugh.

Our ability to lighten up and enjoy a good laugh, even if the laugh is on us, improves our ability to develop and build social capital. In my book, there is something special about the individual who knows how to use humor as an interactional skill.

Let me share one of my best personal humorous stories with you. I once served on a neighborhood community board. The community was located directly across the roadway from a big lake that served as the city's water supply. Ample deer would cross the road all along a stretch that extended as long as the lake, which was about a mile.

Numerous signs that carried the warning DEER CROSSING lined the roadway.

In spite of the numerous signs, however, there were still motorists who hit and killed a number of deer, causing considerable damage to many automobiles. Fortunately, there were no human deaths. The deer accidents were the main topic of discussion one evening at a community board meeting. One of the members of the board, a college professor, spoke up with a suggestion: "Maybe we should consider asking the city to remove the 'deer crossing' signs." That was bad enough, but his next statement took the cake: "That way, there will not be as many deer crossing the roadway." Not one word was uttered, just a lot of smiles and head shakes. That, my friend, is humor.

The hustle and bustle of life has a way of reducing the incidents of humor in our lives. I am reasonably certain that "we don't stop laughing because we grow old, we grow old because we stop laughing."

The fact of the matter is that humor plays a very important role in the quality of life we experience. The root of the word *humor* is "umor." *Umor* means to be fluid, like water. In the same way that water sustains life, humor nourishes life. It helps us survive and thrive in times of change, chaos, and crisis because it

- broadens perspective;

- generates creativity under pressure;

- stimulates a stronger mental and physical presence;

- makes learning more enjoyable;

- enhances our ability to adapt as needed;

- increases retention of information;

- improves spontaneity;

- resolves conflict situations more readily;

- increases effort and productivity; and

- defuses stressful situations.

HUMOR AND PHYSICAL WELL-BEING

Study after study has demonstrated the importance of humor to physical well-being. Having a good old-fashioned belly laugh several times a day can add years to life and life to years. Laughter has been described as "internal jogging" for the following reasons:

- Increases heart rate
- Boosts energy level
- Decreases blood pressure
- Stimulates the overall immune system
- Increases production of T-cells (aids the immune system)
- Stimulates the flow of beta-endorphins (powerful pain suppressors) to the brain
- Improves breathing rate
- Improves natural healing powers
- Increases overall sense of well-being

A funny bone is a great thing to have up your sleeve in dealing with others. Use humor judiciously.

SMILE

Do you have a cheerful face? What can you say about your smile? A smile is a universal language.

Check out these pearls of wit and wisdom that I have collected over the years:

- A smile is an inexpensive way to improve your looks.
- A lot of things are set straight by the curve of a smile.
- The shortest distance between us is about a smile long.
- Smiles are a great investment, for they never go up in price or down in value.

- If you spend most of your younger life smiling, when you get older the wrinkles will be in the right place.

Why Work Overtime?

To send a smile out others' way
Brings thirteen muscles into play;
To think a frown will help us thrive,
Then muscles used will number sixty-five.
Why then should we work overtime?
Is the biggest question on my mind.

—Author Unknown

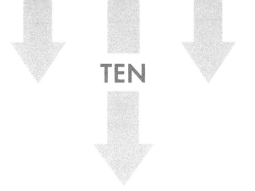

TEN

THE GOLDEN RULE RULES

To get along, we need a pattern of sharing,
A reliance on each other, a premium on caring.
Regardless of where we go or what we do,
We rely on others to help see us through.

—Author Unknown

I enjoy watching geese. They are the epitome of cooperation and leadership. Have you ever observed a flock of geese as they head south for the winter or back north for the summer? They fly in a V formation. They fly this way because, as each bird flaps its wings, it creates an uplift for the bird that is immediately behind it. The whole flock adds at least two-thirds greater flying range than if each bird flew on its own. Geese know instinctively that working together is essential. When the lead goose gets tired, that goose rotates back in the formation (normally to the end of the formation) and each goose moves up.

When a goose gets sick and falls out of formation, two other geese will follow the sick goose to the ground, providing assistance and protection. They stay with the sick goose until that goose is either able to fly again or perishes. The two helpers then launch out to catch up with their original flock or join another group.

We humans are essentially dependent creatures. Human greatness normally involves the roles of many. I like to think that the greatest source of earthly strength we have is each other. We do not lose ourselves by serving others—we find ourselves. We never know how much we are truly worth to ourselves until we know how much we are truly worth to others.

It appears to me that the longer we live, the more we should come to realize that if we want to help ourselves, we can only do so by helping others. In the long run, the Golden Rule rules.

> If nobody cared just a little for you,
> And nobody thought much of me;
> If we all stood alone in the battle of life,
> What kind of world would this be?

—Author Unknown

ENCOURAGEMENT WORKS BEST

An army sergeant wanted to see just how much psychological factors entered into motivation and, ultimately, performance. He divided his squad as equally as possible into two halves based on physical, mental, and emotional capabilities. Their task would be to complete an obstacle course in a certain length of time.

He called the first group together. Addressing them, he said, "Men, you are about to participate in a supreme test of strength, stamina, and mental agility. It will be beyond anything you have ever done before. Not all of you will finish. And of those who do, don't expect to break the time standard we have established for the competition. And finally, please don't feel bad if you fail to do well."

This first group headed toward the obstacle course with a mixture of emotion and checkered confidence. Most did not finish for varied reasons, as Sarge had suggested. Of those who did finish, none beat the time standard.

As the first group was being escorted away from the course, group two was brought in. The sergeant called the group together and told them, "Men, you are about to participate in a supreme test of strength, stamina, and mental agility. It will be beyond anything you have ever done before. But there is no doubt in my mind that you are ready to tackle the obstacle course and do exceedingly well. I expect every one of you to complete the course and beat the time standard."

With that encouragement, the second group attacked the course with optimism and enthusiasm. Everyone in the group finished the course, with over half of them beating the time standard. The sergeant had proven his point on two counts: give people a larger concept of themselves and they will rise to meet your expectations; and the more you expect of others, the more they will come to expect of themselves. Not a bad legacy for any leader of people.

There are varied forms of encouragement. Opportunities to be an encourager abound in many different directions.

For example, most people somewhere along the way experience pains of the heart. Over time, they build solid emotional walls to protect themselves. They learn to cover their hurts and disappointments with false smiles and cheerful actions. No doubt, there are many hurting people around us who need to be comforted and consoled. For someone who is hurting, we can convey a message of support and bonding that can make positive deposits into that person's emotional account. The nicest thing we can give to others today is something to feel important about.

But our role is not always just for those with obvious signs of discomfort. Often the less obvious shared glances and unspoken thoughts are from those seeking comfort for troubled hearts and hidden fears. There are countless folks all around us who are desperately hungry for someone to offer a kind word.

How good are you at offering encouragement? Out there in your world today, you may be the one person who can make another person's world a whole lot better. Often, during the course of a day, a word of praise, an expression of thanks, or a show of appreciation may keep someone going. Today take time to help bring out the best that's in at least one person. Your encouragement might spur that person on to new heights.

And don't forget about those loved ones in your life. Do you offer them a caring ear and an encouraging word when one is needed? Loved ones who are discouraged don't need critics. They hurt enough. They don't need more of "do this" or "do that." What they need is support. They need someone to walk beside them and encourage them. They need to experience the warmth of your heart and to be blessed by your words. They need the very best you. Blessed are those who speak words of encouragement.

Life-Enhancement Message

A real measure of the kind of person you are is how you encourage someone who can do little or nothing for you, except appreciate you for who you are.

THE ART OF OVERLOOKING

What quality in human character do you consider to be the most admirable in dealing with people? For me, it is the quality of overlooking. It is a virtue that sweetens and glorifies life.

The art of overlooking is a very important and valuable art to cultivate. Here is an interesting story about what happened to two brothers, centuries ago, who were convicted of stealing sheep. As part of their penalty for this offense, they were branded on the forehead with the letters *ST*, for "sheep thief." After serving some prison time, the two brothers were released. One brother, unable to bear the stigma of being an ex-convict, moved to a foreign land. But people would constantly ask him about the strange letters. Since he did not want to tell them the reason for the letters, he would simply pick up and move to another city. For years, he wandered restlessly, full of bitterness, and died a lonely, destitute man. He was buried in a forgotten grave.

The other brother said, "I can't run away from the fact that I stole sheep. I will return to my hometown and win back the respect of my neighbors and myself." As the years passed he built a reputation of honesty and integrity. He did marvelous things in the village. The older he got, the more those who knew him practiced the art of overlooking. One day in his golden years, a stranger saw the man with the letters *ST* branded on his forehead. He proceeded to ask a native villager what the *ST* signified. "It happened a great many years ago," said the native villager. "I don't know for sure, but I think the letters are an abbreviation for *saint*."

Life-Enhancement Message

There is a past in every saint's present. There is a future in every sinner's past.

Dr. Frank Crane described the art of overlooking as being "high-souled, rising above pettiness and mean spiritedness."

No one will claim that the art of overlooking is easy. When we feel we have been done wrong, thoughts of retaliation arise. Our first impulse is to strike back, to get "an eye for an eye." It has been my experience that the more we try to get even, the more uneven our lives become.

There is a lot of wisdom in these words of an unknown author:

Wouldn't we all be better off
If the good that is in us all
Were the only thing about us
That we all bothered to recall?

Wouldn't it be great if we told
Each other of the good we see—
I know something good about you;
You know something good about me?

APATHY

What quality in human character do you consider to be the least admirable when it comes to involvement with people? Experience would indicate that there are numerous reasons why people fail to assist others who could use a lift. But in my book, the one that sits right near the top is a condition called apathy. Apathy is the fatal flaw in getting things done for others.

We always had a small number of Hispanic players on each of the ball clubs I played on during my professional career. I felt on many occasions that the other players had a feeling of apathy when it came to mixing with the Hispanic players. Quite possibly the language barrier was the biggest culprit. It was difficult to intermingle with those you could not understand. Part of my motivation for taking Spanish in college was to enhance my interaction with the Hispanic players.

My first full season as a pro baseball player, in 1960, found me in Billings, Montana. About a third of the way through the season, my roommate was released from the team. At the same time, Hector Acosta joined the team. Hector was from South America, spoke no English, and was black.

The unwritten policy at that time was for whites to room with whites and for blacks to room with blacks. Hector's arrival created an imbalance in this formula. So I told the team's general manager that I would room with Hector on road trips.

The communication gap made it rather difficult for us to have a meaningful conversation. I did my best to teach Hector a few words of English. There was one phrase I taught him that he latched on to immediately: "Ham and eggs." He ordered ham and eggs every meal. It took me several weeks to teach him to expand his menu. Ham and eggs were fine with him.

I presume I could have shown a great deal more apathy toward Hector. It wasn't an easy situation for both of us off the playing field. But on the playing field our play kept getting better and better. I told Hector he was my good-luck charm. This term became the basis for his first sentence: "I Luis good-luck charm." A wonderful memory.

Here's my take on apathy: Apathy truly is the art of making sure nothing happens. The stronger apathy gets, the less we feel we need to do anything.

Apathy is all around us. It is contagious. It is easy to catch, and it's painless. I sense the spreading of apathy has a lot to do with the diminishing effects of communication skills. One obvious thing about apathy is that it can rapidly spread over a wide area. As more and more people catch it, the more each person feels it belongs to someone else.

Another obvious thing about apathy is the warm glow of nothingness it gives. The temptation is to leave it alone and it will go away, but it tends to hang around so long as this attitude is prevalent. Apathy demands a special treatment, for it will not go away alone.

It may be hard for a confirmed person who suffers from apathy to start treatments and continue with the cure until apathy is permanently gone. But once started, half the cure is won.

So here's the treatment: it starts with a good dose of involvement, followed by long periods of action. Action will be its own reward when apathy is no longer in place.

You appear to be a person who has left apathy out in the cold. Give yourself a pat on the back for doing something when those around you are doing little to nothing. Action that benefits others creates an inner glow that leaves you with a happy feeling of joy.

Apathy has no place in the life of someone who has the Golden Rule at heart. There is at least one person or one charitable project in every community that someone can be involved in, and contribute energy, time, and talent to. That sounds like you, doesn't it?

SUSPEND WITH COMPARISONS

Do you want to know one of the reasons why some may feel like they are barely making it? They constantly compare themselves to others. They tend to believe others have a better career path, make more money, enjoy a happier marriage, or have a more satisfying life than they do. Envy and jealousy have become their hallmark.

Too many of us keep our focus on what others have got or have done. The belief that others have more is no more than an illusion.

Think with me about this statement: Whatever we focus on in the behavior of others probably lies hidden within ourselves. When we talk about how we like the way others do something, it probably means that we believe we have that same potential within ourselves. No doubt, the same holds true when we downplay what others do well. We are simply projecting what lies dormant within ourselves that we have failed to utilize.

A big reason why we display envious feelings is that we really don't have an accurate grasp of ourselves. We fail to take the time to establish a standard for how we conduct our daily activities: Do you have a standard by which you can gauge your best? Keep in mind that the key person in this determination is you. Your standard for doing your best has nothing to do with others. You will never achieve success by the standards of others. Doing your best according to your personal standards are the only standards that hold up on a daily basis.

I have come to believe that the only true comparison that counts is the one we make with who we are today and who we desire to be in the future. This is the only one that will have staying power over the long haul.

HOW TO HANDLE "NO"

In the arena of living with others, there are always rough patches in bringing them around to our way of thinking, joining our cause, or following our directions. Others saying no is a standard procedure in the real world.

"No" comes in many forms and in many ways, but it always sounds the same. It always hits us between the eyes. That's because we all want to be liked. We all want to be accepted. That's part of the human condition. But, as Dr. Wayne Dyer reminds us, although rejection is a part of life, "rejection can be, and should be, a very temporary condition."

The key is to understand that it is not so much the rejection that we fear as it is the results of rejection. A sound way to go right through the rejection that we receive and stay the course is to work with the following:

- In any role that involves people there is always some rejection that you must expect and accept. Accept the fact that being rejected has happened, does happen, and will continue to happen. Once you accept this vital truth, you can begin to live with it.

- Don't blame yourself or assume something is wrong with you when someone rejects your idea or thought. A no to you is not a no about you! When people turn you down, they are rejecting an idea or a thought, not you. Just let it hurt for a little bit if you must, then forget it and get on with what is next.

- What is a no anyway? Is it an answer? Or a question? Isn't it a question from someone who is anxious for you to provide enough reasons so they can agree with your point of view?

- Try to find the basis for the rejection. "Obviously, you have a reason for feeling the way you do. Do you mind if I ask you what it is?" is a way to get feedback to help you understand the other person's thinking and feelings.

- For years in my training of salespeople, I reminded them to "believe in the law of averages—that each no brings you that much closer to a yes." Rejection doesn't mean never, it just means that you haven't gotten to yes yet.

- Learn this important lesson: If you are not receiving some form of rejection, the chances are good that you are seldom putting yourself into a position where you can be rejected. Don't let your expectations of being rejected keep you from seeking out new opportunities and challenges.

- Ask yourself, *What is the worst thing that can happen?* That's right: someone can say no. But please understand that the nos you hear only become final and fatal when you let them paralyze your ability to approach people. Have the mind-set that each no you hear is just a step closer to a yes.

ELEVEN

LEARNING TOUCHES THE FUTURE

I signed a professional baseball contract shortly after graduating from high school. A very important stipulation was attached to the signing: I promised my mother I would get a college degree.

Ten years after receiving my high school diploma, I earned my college diploma. Can you imagine the fun I have had over the years discussing my ten-year college tenure?

Before you write me off as a dumb jock, let me explain. I was only able to attend classes sporadically. Troy University (present name), where I attended college, was on a quarter system, not a semester system. Some years I was able to attend classes for two quarters; other years, only one. No online classes in those days. I did this over the course of my baseball career.

I mention this as a prelude to our discussion on learning. Preparation and learning are the key differences between our present and a brighter future.

KEEP LEARNING

I have discovered that nothing fails like success if it keeps us from developing new and better habits of performance. One of the worst mental traps we can get into is to feel that we have learned all we need to know. After doing something for an extended period of time, we have a tendency to think that we know it all. This obviously leaves us less open to new information that could influence our future, doesn't it?

I can assure you that about the time we think we have gotten a good handle on things and start to take them for granted, something is going to happen to make us realize that we don't have quite as good a grip as we first thought. You best reread that sentence.

Don't you think it is strange how much we have to know before we know how little we do know?

Some of the best things we learn will be learned after we believe we have learned all the things we need to know. One thing is for sure: the more we know, the more we realize how much there is to know.

That brings us to the one thing that we need to know for sure: We are not ever going to know all we need to know about what we ought to know. Continuous learning will be a big factor in cultivating a great present and a superb future.

Years ago, in another book (*Up Your Attitude*, Upword Press, 1985), I wrote, "Our ability to learn, grow, and get better is not marked by years—it is marked by a state of mind. Years will weather the hide, but to quit learning will weather the soul. Knowledge and skills know no age; they never grow old."

There is an old statement that reads, "Learning gives you something to fall back on." That's partially true. The real theme behind learning is to have something to move us forward, as well as to have something to fall back on. Would you agree?

There is a notable conclusion that we can draw from learning: the real purpose of learning is not knowing but using what we know.

> If we keep doing what we have always done, we won't keep getting the results we have always gotten. That's because skills, methods, and tactics need to be constantly upgraded to keep up with the changes happening around us and within us.

IS GOOD ENOUGH GOOD ENOUGH?

It has been my experience that we don't fall into a performance rut, we are coaxed into it one little slip at a time. Little by little our performance slips until we find ourselves running wide open just to try to stay even.

Nothing fails like success if it keeps us from developing new and better habits of performance. Isn't there, however, a tendency, when we are doing something reasonably well, to not concern ourselves with making any forward-looking improvements and adjustments?

The question before us is, Is good enough good enough if better is possible? I think when we put a limit on how much we think we can improve, we have put a limit on how much we will improve. But improvement doesn't always dictate a physical change. Often the best improvement emanates from changing our attitude.

There is no place where we suddenly become great at anything that we do. To become great means we understand the pain that comes from constantly working toward improvement.

Life-Enhancement Message

Good is the enemy of better, and better is the enemy of best, and good enough is not good enough if better is possible. It appears to me that the best way to make our good better is to work to make our better best. So keep on until your good is better and your better is best.

—Adapted from several sources

RETROFITTING

Retrofitting is a useful term to describe our need to continuously make positive shifts in the way we perform. It refers to our ability to upgrade and retool our old habits into new and more effective ways of performing tasks.

A life well lived is a life of continual retrofitting. We have already determined that we cannot say there is nothing more to learn, no more skills to develop, no more problems to be dealt with, no more new tactics and techniques to try, regardless of what we do. We should never fear making appropriate adjustments in the way we perform our daily tasks and duties.

A retrofitting mentality helps us adjust to the transformation happening around us. It keeps us on our toes to actively seek out beneficial modifications in what we are doing. Retrofitting sits at the core of our ability to move beyond the ways we have been doing things when they can no longer guarantee a high level of productivity.

Many factors can keep us from seeking better ways to perform, but one that stands out is overcoming the inertia caused by age. As we become more chronologically gifted, we increasingly tend to look for the easy way out. More and more we reject activities that call for learning new or different ways of performing our daily tasks.

Let me share with you an idea that can keep the "change mechanism" in working order: Make a conscious effort to periodically do routine things differently. It might be something as insignificant as changing which leg you first put into a pair of pants or slacks.

One of my favorites is consciously changing my shaving routine. One day I might start on the left side; the next day, on the right. I make it a priority to consciously think about doing insignificant things in a different way. I really believe this makes me more conscious of finding methods to do more significant tasks in a better way.

As a friend once told me, it's good for us to change our minds on occasion, just to see if they still work. It doesn't hurt to alter the "normal" way we do something on occasion. Give it a try.

Life-Enhancement Message

A quality education, in the long run, is never expensive, but over a lifetime the price of ignorance is always expensive.

ROOM FOR IMPROVEMENT

The biggest room for any of us is the room for improvement. But there is a world of difference between having a desire to upgrade and setting out with a plan for making development a reality.

We accomplish little in life when we wait for all the possible road-blocks to be overcome before we embark on a journey to improve. The future is always uncertain, but having a game plan for progress will make the future less uncertain than it otherwise would be.

What would you say about your ability to develop a game plan for improvement? Do you need to muster some mental toughness to make it a reality?

Learning is a process. Skillfulness is a result of the process. Expertise is established through learning upgrades that lead to more sustainable skills. The more we learn about doing something, the fewer surprises and mysteries we encounter in the future. Over time, everything becomes either more apparent or suggestive of something else. This in turns leads to another viable learning experience . . . and then another.

Expertise is never static. It is stimulated by instructive behavior that continually seeks ways to bring advancement to what we do. The challenge is learning how to become highly proficient with the least expenditure of time and the greatest degree of dependability. Instinctively, selecting the correct action at the right time under the existing circumstances is the basis for developing and expanding, and building a base of expertise.

It has been my experience that the learning process is best served through being attuned to the originality of today. Concentrate on making incremental progress daily. This thought progression leaves the obscurities of the future and the boredom of the present at the door. The now moment is always the best learning moment, wouldn't you think?

ROUTE TO IMPROVEMENT

All of us need to upgrade somewhere.

I think the message is fairly evident: Constant enhancement and improvement should be our standard of performance. But the process of improvement is tied to the desire to improve.

Let me tell you about a former roommate of my mine in the St. Louis Cardinals organization who went on to a Hall of Fame career. We will call him Bobby Winkler.

Bobby could hit a baseball as well as anyone I ever played with, but he had a difficult time finding a place to play on defense. In those days, there was no designated hitter like they have today in the American League of Major League Baseball. He would have been perfect for that role because he would not have had to play defense.

Early in his career Bobby's focus, as a whole, was on hitting the baseball. He rarely spent time working to improve his defense, although numerous coaches attempted to work with him.

Why would he fear working to upgrade his defense? Good question.

It seems that the more others talked to him about making a concerted effort to improve, the less time he spent working at it. Closer observation demonstrated that Bobby absolutely feared to be wrong. Admitting that he was not very good on defense was something he simply could not handle.

About halfway through the season, Bobby was leading the league in hitting. A Cardinal farm team that was a classification above the level where we were playing needed to add a player to their roster. But it wasn't Bobby who got called up (baseball's term for advancement). It was another player who was not as good a hitter as Bobby, but was a better all-around player.

This was Bobby's wake-up call. He just couldn't fathom that someone other than himself would be advanced. He voiced this thought many times. My answer to him was, "Bobby, you're the only one who can change that perception."

Surprisingly, Bobby got the message. He began putting in extra time with the coaches, working to improve his fielding. Slowly his skill level got better and better. And so did his confidence.

Bobby made a miraculous turnaround during the second half of that season. He found the mental fortitude to seek help. This brought improvement in his ability to play well when he was on defense.

Bobby simply had to look in the mirror to see the source of his problem. The blessing was that Bobby did find the courage to deal with the source. Within two years, he was playing at a high level in the major leagues.

Bobby had stepped up to home plate and hit the ball out of the park. It wouldn't have happened without expanding his overall game.

Determining what route to take in getting our improvement program moving is our first priority. We begin the process by looking at the skill-set level we would like to achieve, then looking at where we are now. Between these two points is the substance of our game plan for development.

Then we need to ask this important question: *What am I willing to give up in order to make room for progress?*

Two thoughts to consider here are (1) every time we let go of something that limits us, we create room for something better; and (2) the longer we put off making enhancements in our skills and techniques, the longer it will take when we get around to it.

As our game plan develops, we learn that progress is often slow and tedious—often from one plateau to another—which means we have to undergo much trial and success to reach an efficient level of performance.

How do we make the expansion of possibilities more defined and easier to do?

I think it is imperative that our attention be directed toward the positive aspects of what is to be gained, rather than focusing on the negatives of what we are giving up. Keep thinking about what the newly acquired skills and techniques will mean in terms of increased performance and greater growth possibilities.

THE PLATEAU

Skills development is not straight up. The rate of improvement can reach a level of little or no change, notably after some highly effective growth. Developing skills occurs in stages—or as the experts say, "from one plateau to the next plateau."

Reaching a plateau is a natural part of the learning process. A plateau doesn't mean that we are stymied in acquiring new knowledge. It simply means we have to digest the development we have made before we can work through to new heights of advancement. A plateau also may mean that after being exposed to the same type of knowledge and skill development for an extended period of time, we no longer sense a challenge. As a result, we settle into a routine, and as a consequence, we fail to reap the same benefits as we had done previously.

Think of a plateau as a beginning, not an ending. This is the start that can lead to being committed to move on to a higher level. There is an elementary mind-set that can make improvement possibilities more defined when you are in the midst of a plateau. This mind-set calls for you to keep searching and working for ways to sharpen techniques, hone skills, and improve attitudes. With each step, you learn a little more, grow more confident, become a little better, and keep moving beyond the current plateau, for the greater fulfillment of what is on the other side.

MONOTASKING

My friend George Schultz constantly kids me about his ability to multitask. "Hey, Lou, I'm a great multitasker," he expresses with a broad grin. "I can walk, talk, and chew gum all at the same time," he adds with a big, hearty laugh.

We all realize that multitasking is a bit more complicated than that practiced by George. When it comes to letting go and making changes, multitasking tends to create information overload. So what can we do differently? The answer is monotasking.

Monotasking is the ability to embrace doing one thing at once. It makes little difference if the adjustments we need to make are personal, professional, or both. Monotasking can assist us in making it happen quicker and more correctly.

Whatever the task, consciously discipline yourself to work on one part of it at a time. Develop a monotasking routine that reminds you to do certain things at certain times. The route to development involves improving one skill, or even one step in the execution of a skill, at a time. When that skill has been mastered, it will spur action toward mastering the next skill, and then the next one.

Skills advancement takes time. Now don't expect to fully develop a skill or tactic overnight. Earlier, we saw that research shows it takes a minimum of twenty-one days to feel comfortable performing a new skill. Then it will take another three weeks to make the skill or technique a significant part of your regular routine. But the moment our focus is on a single fault and practice is directed toward improving that single skill, progress begins to show before you know it. The key is monotasking.

Just for the record, it takes us significantly longer to get back on track when we are constantly moving back and forth from one thing to the next. Monotasking makes it easier on the brain. The brain processes best through the contemplative practice of doing one thing at a time.

Just remember, once you know what you should do, there is only one way to get it done right: monotask. Do one thing at once.

EXERCISE PATIENCE

When seeking ways and means of expanding your skills base, understand progress normally moves slowly. You must appreciate that you cannot conquer everything at once. Discovering and growing take time.

The challenge is that if most people don't receive instant success or gratification, they get discouraged. They want what they want now, and if they don't get it now, they walk away and quit. That hasn't been your history, has it?

The one big difference that exists between those who demonstrate the desire to stay the course and those who give up and go on to something else is patience. The lack of patience is one of the major reasons why a significant number of people fail to succeed.

Too many people are looking for someone to give them three easy steps on how to be successful at what they do, and they want these steps to produce enormous progress right away. But meaningful performance modification takes time, and time takes patience.

Once we have fully implemented behavior to make changes in step with our purpose and values in life, we need to give those actions time to materialize. We didn't get to the point of needing corrective action yesterday, and effective change isn't going to be visible overnight. Patience, my friend. Patience.

When we are concerned if something is going to work or not, the very best thing to do is to give it time to work. It is imperative that we give what we have done a fair chance to make a difference in our lives. Sit tight. Be patient. Wait.

I realize you may become frustrated and feel like quitting because you question if making effective changes is worth the time and effort. If the lack of patience sounds like one of your challenges, please don't feel like you're alone. But to join the ranks of highly successful people, you have to grasp the fact that patience is often needed to move the needle.

Patience is a learned skill. If you are committed to making quality adjustments in your performance base, patience will be at the forefront of making it a reality. Just remember: the key to patience is strategic waiting, which is all the positive things you do in the meantime.

STRATEGIC WAITING

The power of patience is the result of invisible dividends. When you practice patience, time is on your side. You cannot hasten your destiny. The key is to practice strategic waiting.

Do the best you can and let results work themselves out. Practice strategic waiting.

When you have a solid plan for change that has been well thought out, one in which you have taken all the variables into consideration, why shouldn't you give it a chance to work? Practice strategic waiting.

Refrain from jumping in and making frequent adjustments. As you proceed with your change pattern for a period of time, you must be careful of giving up before the modifications have time to work. Practice strategic waiting.

Back off and digest what has happened, allowing yourself to remain as patient and determined as is humanly possible. Practice strategic waiting.

Let your inner consciousness take over and provide a platform that will take you right over the rough spots. Practice strategic waiting.

After a while, as the adjustments you make become second nature, a sixth sense will develop to solidify your understanding of what you are doing and the progress you are making. You will have succeeded because you will have made strategic waiting a part of your regular routine.

DISCIPLINE IS THE KEY

If we are going to have patience and be able to practice strategic waiting, we must be disciplined. The word *discipline* comes from the Latin word *discipulus*, which means "pupil" or "learner."

Normally, when we think of discipline, we think of punishment. But training and correction are the primary ingredients of discipline. Practicing discipline allows us to be in a position to learn. We have to discipline ourselves for the purpose of utilizing patience and practicing strategic waiting in the application and fulfillment of what we learn.

Discipline can teach us how to exercise patience in the face of the multitude of events and situations we experience daily. On many occasions we need discipline in the areas of thoughts, words, temper, and time. The reason why so many of our good resolves have not been realized is that we have never learned how to discipline ourselves. Discipline takes work and sustained daily effort. Discipline takes constant practice.

What areas of your daily efforts need a good dose of discipline?

We aren't born with discipline; it's a learned behavior. Just like any other behavioral skill you want to master, discipline requires daily practice and repetition. Adam Sicinski wrote that "self-discipline is more specifically about your ability to control your desires and impulses in an attempt to stay focused (for long enough) on what needs to get done."

I believe that commitment to a vision or goal will serve us well in developing discipline. We must be fully committed to doing whatever it takes to minimize our weaknesses and eliminate temptations if we are to reach beyond where we are to hang our hat on something more productive.

What I hope you hear me saying is that we must simply possess some good, old-fashioned willpower that arises from the depths of our being. The amount of willpower each one of us acquires is determined by strong-held personal beliefs. If we place no internal limits on our capabilities of continually developing willpower, we will exhaust all means of exercising self-control and self-discipline.

In a nutshell, our internal conceptions about willpower and self-control determine how much discipline we utilize. If we truly believe we can do it, then we will give ourselves an extra boost of motivation toward making our learning goals a reality.

CONSTRUCTIVE CRITICISM

The probability of criticism comes with the territory in any meaningful endeavor. This is much more noticeable in the daily hustle and bustle of doing tedious chores and tasks. I can promise you that it is very evident at the professional sports level.

It is my personal opinion that the only type of criticism that can bring a real element of improvement is constructive criticism. Learning opportunities that are spiced with an element of constructive criticism are designed to make us better, not bitter.

If you are like me, you have had your share of negative criticism. I want to share a story of a time when I was criticized but it carried no future consequences. In fact, it created some very humorous moments over the years.

The year was 1983. My mother, three of my sisters, and I went to Mobile, Alabama, for a tryout for the TV program *Family Feud*. Not being a big TV-watching fan, I knew little about the show.

I arrived at the hotel where the tryouts were being conducted, and there must have been a thousand people there. This was obviously big stuff.

I had been in New Orleans on business, and I arrived wearing a three-piece suit. I was the only one with a suit on in the place. My sisters were beside themselves, insisting that I needed to be anything but businesslike for this audition.

I eased out to my car and got my old, tattered rain hat. I wore it into the audition, and I am still convinced to this day that it helped us procure one of the spots for a trip to Hollywood. We were soon off on a trip to spend a week on the left coast.

We saw most of the Hollywood sites during the week. Then it came time to tape the show. Folks, I was bad, real bad. I did not answer one question correctly. The highlight of the evening for me—and what I heard about for years—was the question "What do you feed the animals in the zoo?" Mom and my sisters had correct answers to the question. We only needed one more correct answer to be a winner. All the answers bouncing around in my head had been given; then out of my mouth came, "Animal crackers." The laughter that arose from the audience indicated my answer was not good. I can still hear the buzzer signifying an incorrect answer. We didn't win.

After the show, the producer came into the dressing room and proceeded to announce to me, "We have had some bad ones on this show, but you may have been the worse!" Okay. You can laugh. It was not a laughing matter at the time. And it was a long time after the show aired before the kidding subsided.

I don't think we can properly prepare ourselves for building a better future without the ability to handle all kinds of criticism. The lessons, however, are in the constructive criticism. Until we learn how to accept constructive criticism from others, improvement is thwarted.

What is the best way to take constructive criticism in stride? We have to learn to cope, not defend. When we cope with the critical remarks about a performance or behavior, we see those comments for what they are: constructive ways for us to perform better. But when we try to defend our actions and the level of our present performances, we come from a negative base. Instead of focusing on how to get better, we tend to support ineffective ways of performing. The more we defend those poor performances, the longer they will be a part of our daily routine.

When an authority figure has something critical to say about your efforts, look for the good first. Don't fall into the trap of personalizing the comments of others. A criticism *to* you is not always a criticism *about* you—and please don't forget it.

Life-Enhancement Message

It is not the critic who counts; not the man who points out how the strong man stumbles, or where the doer of deeds could have done them better. The credit belongs to the man who is actually in the arena, whose face is marred by dust and sweat and blood, who strives valiantly; who errs and comes short again and again . . . who at the best knows in the end the triumph of high achievement, and who at the worst, if he fails, at least fails while daring greatly, so that his place shall never be with those cold and timid souls who neither know victory nor defeat.
—President Theodore Roosevelt

TWELVE

TIME AND ACTIVITY MANAGEMENT

Your success ratio grows to the extent that your
time and activity management skills grow.

We must have structure in our daily activities to take consistent steps forward. The brain functions more efficiently when activities are structured. Simply put: management of time and workflow activities structures and organizes our thought patterns. This enables us to formulate the most effective ways to maximize our time usage and organizational skills. This in turn helps us to stretch ourselves and reach beyond.

Managing time and activity flow also tends to pull us out of our comfort zones and tap into our deepest resources. It puts us in a better position to assess and measure our regular daily activities and their alignment with our purpose, vision, and goals. And motivation is made easier when we have a significantly better idea of what we want to do and how to accomplish it.

TIME USAGE

Management of activities formulates around how we use our time. Time is the one resource distributed equally to everyone, for each day has the same number of hours, each hour has the same number of minutes, and each minute has the same number of seconds. This will never change.

What changes is how these hours, minutes, and seconds are used. The great paradox of time is that there is nothing more unequal than its usage. Time is worth nothing in and of itself. It is how time is used that puts a value on it.

TIME USAGE MANAGEMENT

Is time management a challenge for you? How can you be more effective in the usage of your time? Need some suggestions? Hopefully, these ideas will help:

- **Clarify objectives.** *What do I need to do today?* Break each day of the week down into three distinct parts: morning, afternoon, and evening. What do you need to be doing in each segment of the day to maximize your time?

- **Schedule your activities.** *What activities need to be done today?* Time management works in reverse—from the future back to the present. Look at what needs to be done to reach beyond, and then plan the best use of your time to get it done.

- **Recognize your productive hours.** *When should I be doing my most important tasks?* Determine the hours when you are highly energized, and attempt to schedule your key appointments during these high-energy periods.

- **Evaluate each activity objectively.** Before you schedule any activity, question whether it is really necessary. Ask yourself, *Will this activity make a significant contribution to the results or enjoyment I want to obtain?*

- **Combine tasks.** *What similar tasks can I group together?* Concentrate on one important thing at a time, but do multiple, less important things in sequences. Learn to divide larger projects into separate stages.

- **Group telephone calls and social media activity.** This practice is known as *time-blocking.* Block out chunks of time on your calendar to focus on completing mass quantities of repetitive tasks. Make as many phone calls or send out as many social media messages as you can at one time to keep your focus. (Another time-saving idea is to tell people what specific time period in the day you prefer to be contacted.)

- **Learn to say no.** The more you do, the more you are going to be asked—and expected—to do. You must learn how to tactfully say no on occasion. Saying no to others on relatively unimportant things is like saying yes for you to have more time to do important things.

- **Set deadlines.** Deadlines serve to offset procrastination—they get you into action. Take a minute to think about the intensity of the last few minutes of the fourth quarter in a close college football game, or how many points are typically scored in the last few seconds of an NBA basketball game. A deadline is a great motivator.

- **Don't postpone difficult chores.** They weigh you down mentally and affect your productivity. Be decisive. –Don't put off making important decisions to tackle important tasks. Then, when you do make them, finish what you start and move on.

WELL-ORGANIZED GAME PLAN

The secret for being well organized is to have

1. a *goal* to provide a vision and a purpose to what we want to do (and be);

2. a *plan* to give us direction for how to do it;

3. a *schedule* to help us determine when to do it; and

4. a *priority* list to aid in determining the most effective use of time to do it.

Having a game plan that entails the above four points makes our future less uncertain and more productive. A game plan helps us step out of our comfort zone and do things that we formerly felt we were incapable of doing. It gets us into the rhythm of things. Then we begin to click and soon accomplish more than we ever imagined we could.

These are the questions you should be asking yourself as you develop your game plan:

- *Where am I intending to go? Unless I know where I am going, how do I know when I have arrived?*

- *How do I plan to get there? Unless I have a legitimate plan for getting the results I want, what are the chances of my obtaining them?*

One of the elementary keys to a successful life is to carefully design a plan to serve as a road map for how to get there. A poorly planned life pattern, if you are lucky, will afford you an opportunity at a redesign. Is that where you are right now?

BENEFITS OF PLANNING

This is not new unless it is new to you: "Plan your work, then work your plan."

Dr. David Dyson has been a friend of mine for almost twenty years. He is a director at Life Leaders Institute in Birmingham, Alabama. David is a consultant and an executive coach for personal, professional, and leadership development. He has assisted countless individuals and organizations in putting systems into place that help plan for a more propitious life.

According to David, "One of life's highest purposes is to be good stewards of our callings, gifts, and talents. We need plans for developing ourselves, solving problems, and achieving results.

In every area of life, plans that include goals and time management, factors of scheduling and prioritizing, help us succeed. Plans create stability and internalize inspiration. Without the benefit of plans, we are like a feather in a windstorm."

The benefits of planning are manifold:

- Provides time awareness.
- Concentrates effort where it counts by proper prioritizing.
- Increases control of direction.
- Prepares in advance what to do and when to do it.
- Helps to react reliably and quickly to change.
- Aids in staying consistently on course.
- Unexpected events are handled with a minimum of delays.
- Assists in working comfortably under pressure.
- Pinpoints areas that show potential trouble.
- Defines strategies within a realistic framework.
- Assists in broadening the field of required actions.
- Gives you confidence—you know where to begin and where you're heading.

WHAT MATTERS IN PLANNING

- **Focus on the now.** Living in the past keeps you fixated on what was done by you or to you rather than what you are capable of doing right now.
- **Think things through.** Imagine the alternatives available and the possible consequences of those actions.

- **Be specific in your needs.** What do you want? Let those around you know about specific, legitimate needs. Don't keep others guessing.

- **Examine assumptions.** Explore possibilities and examine carefully the answers. Utilize patience.

- **Go after what you believe in.** You do not do what you know, you do what you believe about what you know. Go for it!

PRIORITY MANAGEMENT

One of the great lessons of time management is to learn how to prioritize. These suggestions will definitely make your priority decisions better:

- Set your own priorities—don't let others set them for you.

- Make a daily "things to accomplish" list.

- Work from your "things to accomplish" list.

- Keep your "things to accomplish" list simple.

- Break larger or long-term tasks into manageable parts.

- Differentiate between urgent tasks and important ones.

- Make definite appointments; confirm them and keep them.

- Group and perform related tasks together.

- Plan realistically. Anything worthwhile takes longer than expected.

- Establish activities on the basis of importance and urgency. Remember: "What is important is seldom urgent, and what is urgent is seldom important."

- Don't forget to utilize the three *R*s—Rest, Relaxation, and Recreation—to stay balanced. Unsuccessful people can't wait to escape from their unfulfilling lives, whereas successful people use downtime to recharge their batteries for the intensity of the road ahead.

Life-Enhancement Message

Priority management is not an act but a habit.

PRIORITIZING: THE "THINGS TO ACCOMPLISH" LIST

Take time to weigh the activities on your "things to accomplish" list for their relative importance. The following questions are designed to help prioritize your daily tasks on your list:

- *What are my highest priorities to be performed today?*

- *Which will give me the highest return for time invested?*

- *Which tasks will, if left undone, represent the greatest threat to my success?*

- *Which tasks do I consider most vital to making progress today?*

- *Which incomplete tasks from previous days need to be done today?*

- *Which tasks can be done only by me, and no one else?*

- *Which tasks can I get help on to complete ASAP?*

STARTING AND STICKING WITH PRIORITIES

- Visualize yourself completing a task, and vividly see the rewards *you* will receive.

- Avoid pessimists; they tend to discourage you from even trying.

- Fight perfectionism; you don't have to be perfect, just excellent.

- Don't be afraid to make mistakes; they show you what works—and what doesn't.

- Be flexible; evaluate your priorities and adjust your course accordingly.

- Do what you have to do when you have to do what you need to do.

ORGANIZING THOUGHTS

Do you experience difficulty in organizing your thoughts? Take these suggestions to heart:

- Scrutinize what you hear. Be careful of grabbing hold of someone else's opinion and making it your own because it sounds good. Carefully scrutinize, question, or test it before you decide to accept it.

- *Will it work?* Brilliant revelations that bounce off the walls of your mind are only sufficient if they pass the application test.

- Practice discernment. Be definitive about information. Practice defining what will be useful and what will not. Filter out that which does not apply to your mission.

- *I don't know.* If you don't know, say so. As someone so astutely said, "To say 'I don't know' is a sign that you know what you know, and you also know what you don't know."

- Ask questions. There is no such thing as a dumb question, but you may get or give a dumb answer. Don't pretend you know something when you really don't understand it.

- Classify your information. Computers and electronic storage units make it easy to classify your personal thoughts. This greatly enhances your recall abilities.

- "Proprietor of useless information." Many listeners of my radio show kidded me about this one. I was always presented relatively useless information. For example, "How many notches in a dime?" How about 110! Waste little time in acquiring useless general information that you can look up on the Internet at a moment's notice.

- Read and study with a purpose. I rarely read anything without making notes on my computer as I go. I have a purpose in mind. Is that something that will aid you?

- Make learning your daily companion. What information will be beneficial to you today? Remember, you don't know all you need to know about what you should know. So keep on learning.

- Keep your thoughts positive. In the final analysis, this will make the biggest difference in how effective your thoughts will be when applied.

BRAIN MAPPING

The whole idea of this chapter focuses on how important it is for us to have great structure in our lives. Daily success is built on structure. Structure is a form of organization. Organization develops around time and activity management.

One of the things that have been real blessings to me in organizing my activities is the use of brain mapping in structuring how to handle important tasks. A typical brain map revolves around one main theme or topic, which I represent with a small circle in the middle.

Being from the old school, I draw my brain map on an eight-and-a-half-by-eleven-inch piece of paper. Many of you have electronic instruments that you probably would use for brain mapping. A number of software applications on every major platform allow for the easy development and sharing of information.

First, establish the main theme. Write it within the small circle in the center of the page. Once this main theme has been established, draw several larger circles around the main circle. The picture we get here looks like a mother planet attached to numerous larger satellite planets. The larger satellite circles represent actions that need to be taken to achieve the goal in the main circle. If necessary, draw a series of smaller satellite circles that are attached to the larger satellite circles, where you detail the actions to be taken. The brain map begins to take shape as we formulate specific ideas within the series of outer circles. The satellite circles aid us in brainstorming various ways to accomplish the theme in the main circle.

Let's say that the goal in the main circle is to increase marketing efforts. The main circle obviously would be labeled MARKETING. In the satellite circles, we then would describe various ideas and methods that could possibly lead to greater marketing success.

For example, the larger circles could carry labels such as "contact existing clients," "generate new leads," "network with new people," or "improve the product presentation." Once the labels are established, list specific ideas on how to accomplish each.

Let's look at "generate new leads." Within the outlying, smaller circles we would write the detailed actions to be undertaken. This might include contacting ten potential clients via social media, starting a newsletter, or mailing a new product brochure.

Do you see how brain maps can be a powerful way to organize your thoughts? By developing an ongoing brain map for each of your core task functions, you will be able to capture all of those small ideas that randomly pop into your head. You can then use them to create definitive plans of action for achieving greater results.

Two Winning Ends

We have two winning ends;
They have a common link;
With the bottom end we move;
With the top end we think.
And our success depends on
How we maximize their use;
For common sense tells us,
With both we win—one we lose.

—Adapted from an unknown author

THIRTEEN

GOALS TO GROW

I live on the Gulf Coast, and fishing is big here. I am constantly reminded of one thing about fishing boats: one cannot expect a boat full of fish to be brought back in unless the boat is sent out equipped with the intent of accomplishing this task. Sounds elementary, doesn't it? But it is a fact of life that the docks are full of people who have loaded their boats with great dreams and aspirations, but fail to launch them.

Boats sitting in the harbor not only fail to sail, they start to rust and decay. Dreams are washed away when we fail to push our boats away from the docks into the waters that will lead us to a greater destination. There is no guarantee that a decision to launch our boats will result in any great "catch." There is, however, a certainty that if we do send our boats out, we have a reasonable and even greater chance to reach the desirable waters that will increase our odds of reeling in huge rewards.

When those who have gone on to bigger and better things started their life's journey, very few of them knew with unshaken conviction and assurance what they needed to do to get a head start on life. But it didn't take them long to understand that to enjoy any measure of success in life, it would necessitate being definitive on what they wanted to do, why they felt they could do it, and how to do it. This realization placed the accent right on developing a concrete purpose and unyielding vision to plant the seeds from which their goals produced the best growth.

Life-Enhancement Message

It is difficult to get from here to there if you cannot visualize where "there" is. Begin with a vision of the end in mind.

PURPOSE AND VISION

Purpose and vision are rock-solid factors in jump-starting a future. You might ask, *Which comes first: purpose or vision?* Purpose and vision are often debated in terms of order. While they are both important as we go about the task of establishing a blueprint for setting goals, we will talk about purpose first.

Purpose is behind our reasons for existence. It is about our "why." When we have clarity in our purpose, our vision will always have better direction.

Vision is future oriented. It describes what we hope to achieve in the future. Vision includes the basic concept of where we are heading. It serves as a guiding inspiration that portrays the kind of future to which we aspire.

Be honest with yourself: Have you taken the time to slow down and launch the internal search for a real purpose and a forward-looking vision that will be the foundation for your goals? Need some rekindling? Most of us do. Read on.

REKINDLING

I am right at the head of the line of those who have come up short in achieving all of the hopes, dreams, and goals that I established years ago. Sometimes we come up short because of varied circumstances and personal reasons, which are generally of our own making. Other times, there are things beyond our control that create the need to redefine our purpose and vision going forward.

The important thing is that we recognize when we haven't made the kind of progress we hoped to make, and ask, what next? The time may be at hand to rejuvenate the depth and meaning of a well-grounded purpose and a clear vision, or to search anew for a higher level of opportunity that can arise from an expanded purpose and/or a replenished vision.

If this is the station in life where you presently find yourself, I want to encourage you to think in terms of rekindling your purpose and/or vision. I urge you to take the time to write down the reasons why you want to bring your lost hopes and dreams back, or how you can begin anew.

Why is it so important to write them down? First of all, because you have to think about them in order to do this. Secondly, the power of seeing them with your eyes stirs your imagination. Start the process now. Why wait until it may be too late?

The combination of purpose and vision tells a clear, complete, and compelling story—each working together—to assist us in instituting goals that will bring us closer to the kind of people we aspire to be.

DEEP-FELT PURPOSE

A crystal-clear vision arises from a deep-felt purpose for our life's journey. No matter what we do, we can draw a deeper meaning from it with the deliberate and clear intent of a solid purpose.

Let me share with you why I think having a significant purpose is so important. Our purpose is the only constant in life on which we can rely in the face of the varied circumstances and uncontrollable conditions that we encounter. Purpose serves to maximize the impact of and influence things that will make us more industrious and productive, regardless of what life throws at us. Purpose does it better than anything else can. It's the driving force behind our realizing what we can do and become.

Self-growth does not happen without a planned expectation. With a great underlying purpose, our vision does have a specific direction. Our goals are more secure. Our focus is razor sharp. Our potential is more pronounced and more attainable. A sense of purpose enables us to connect with our mission and be more passionate about it.

I was drafted out of the St. Louis Cardinals organization by the New York Yankees in the winter of 1964. No other franchise or sports brand is as famous as the Yankees. My dad, Buddy, was an enormous Yankee fan and was excited over my going to the Yankees, to say the least. Spring Training of 1965 found me in the same clubhouse with the likes of Mantle, Maris, Ford, Howard, Kubek, and Richardson, some of the greatest Yankee players of all time. I was excited to be there.

I must admit that I grew up being anything but a Yankees fan. But I learned really quickly that you should never be critical of the hand that has your paycheck in it.

My locker in the clubhouse was directly across from Hall of Famer Mickey Mantle. Mickey's better days as a player were behind him.

I watched him daily as he placed a wrap around each leg, extending from his ankle to his thigh. It was evident his legs hurt badly, yet he played, and played well. One morning as we were dressing for practice, Mickey noticed that I had older equipment: glove, shoes, etc. In those days, baseball clubs did not supply these items to players; it was the player's responsibility to procure them.

Mickey asked if I had a contract with one of the major baseball equipment suppliers, like Rawlings or Spalding. They supplied players with equipment for their endorsement. I expressed to Mickey that I did not have a contract. After returning from the practice field later that day, there was a complete supply of new equipment, including a warm-up jacket, at my locker. When I thanked Mickey for his assistance, he told me, "Kid, being a Yankee means going first class."

Isn't our real purpose in life "to go first class"?

A sense of purpose is important because it aids in tapping into our "first-class" reserves of energy, desire, and courage. When we have a definitive purpose, we are more apt to concentrate our efforts on what matters the most.

It is from the reality base of a genuine purpose that we formulate the framework for a crystal-clear vision that will set the tone for life-fulfilling goals. This fortified purpose will serve to inspire us to become something special.

Life-Enhancement Message

*A sense of purpose is our compass on the road on which
we travel; it enriches the journey we undertake and creates
a destination with more certainty and assurance.*

SCRIPT A PURPOSE

Do I hear you asking, *How do I establish a greater sense of purpose in my life?* Think of your purpose as being your mission statement. Fill in the blanks: *Why do I want to be____? Why do I want to do_____? Why do I want to have____?* The answers to these questions hold the purpose for living life well. They are guideposts to achieving personal fulfillment along life's pathway.

My personal belief is that purpose evolves from doing things that come naturally to us. "Develop your play around your strengths," was a reminder from one of my coaches years ago.

Do you play to your strengths? We rarely aspire toward something we have little talent in because it's not a natural fit. Utilizing the abilities and assets we are innately good at doing is at the core of finding and empowering our purpose. In chapter 8, we took a look at the question "What is your 'that'?" As you recall, your "that" is part of your personal brand. When you have a handle on your "that," you will have a much better handle on playing to your strengths.

Some very successful people I have known established a path to success early on. They worked to their strengths. But not everyone has that kind of insight, do they? The more natural path is to kind of feel our way until we, hopefully, find our footing. We may have to work our way through the maze created by self-doubt before achievement becomes a possibility.

One thing is for sure: we cannot sit back hoping and wishing that the next bit of action will be the magic genie that will unleash our great potential and make our dreams come true. It doesn't work that way. My point is that we are better at what we do when we have the natural talent to do it. We have a running head start with that attitude.

With the added value of passion and enthusiasm, we are well placed and better equipped to tackle our greatest challenges. A strong sense of purpose makes that possible.

VISUALIZE IN YOUR IMAGINATION

It is what we visualize that forms a base from which we make a determination about what we are passionate about. On the great screen in our minds, we can envision ourselves in the act of realizing our hopes, dreams, and goals, long before they materialize. We can visualize ourselves doing the things that need to be done to enjoy a future of fulfillment.

How close are you to becoming the person your vision dictates that you aspire to become? It is not unusual to suffer from blurred vision about the future. Sometimes our lenses get clouded over. Countless of us may stagger around and bump into a lot of hurdles and obstacles before settling on a workable life vision. I know. I have been there myself.

It has been my experience that the most optimal route to arrive at a superior future destination is to visualize it in our imagination. When we visualize the kind of world in which we want to live, it becomes easier to establish the framework for how we can create it and then live it. Sooner or later, we all discover that the imagination is the workshop where the construction of a rewarding future begins.

Have you thought about the potential the imagination holds in developing the future? It allows us to explore the possibilities and probabilities along life's path long before we begin the journey. It lays the pavement over which our reality ride will eventually carry us. On this visualized trip we can see ourselves in the act of being and doing something special long before it becomes a reality. We can actually imagine the things that need to be done to reach the pinnacle of a successful destination.

VISUALIZE SUCCESS

When we hold a mental picture of ourselves doing and being something better, long enough and consistently enough, it trains the mind to expect and work at what it takes to be something greater. Creating a mental picture of being something more than what we presently are molds our minds into seeking a higher purpose in life.

What are you visualizing for your next step in life? When you possess a clear and determined vision, you're more apt to set in motion the wheels of transformation. Action has a way of following a well-designed mental plan. What we visualize is what we tend to accomplish.

My friend Brad Vegas is a prime example of having a vivid imagination that developed into a winning vision. In the late 1980s, Brad had a vision that would lead him to become known as the "grandfather of artificial rocks." Brad developed a glass-reinforced artificial cement rock for indoor/outdoor waterfalls that became the standard for the industry.

It is particularly interesting how Brad came to develop his concept for artificial rocks. He would personally hike up in the mountains to find rocks of specific styles and designs. Brad would spray the rocks of choice with liquid rubber. After the rubber hardened, Brad removed the newly created mold from the rocks. He made molds of various designs for both indoor and outdoor waterfalls. Brad then put plaster inside the molds and sculpted the rock look-alikes.

Now, Brad was ready to make a major decision. Armed with a vision and a desire to manufacture his version of artificial rocks, he left a well-paying job in Austin, Texas, and moved to Tampa, Florida. He selected Tampa because the Florida market appeared to be a great place to market these artificial rocks. However, he immediately ran into a major hurdle. A six-figure monetary settlement that he expected from his previous company never materialized. The company filed bankruptcy and Brad never received the money.

To make matters worse, Brad had already borrowed a significant amount of money to get his business kicked off. Over the course of the next two years, Brad went from bank to bank to pay off existing small loans. During this time, Brad continued to develop his vision of a business to manufacture the artificial rocks. His bedroom of choice was in a warehouse that he had rented to establish a manufacturing facility. Brad was literally living hand to mouth.

Finally, Brad found a bank that believed in his vision. The bank loan gave him a two-year window to get his company up and running.

Soon the company, Waterfall Creations, was manufacturing the kind of artificial rocks he had envisioned. Brad's business grew rapidly. Within five years, he paid off his debt and made the decision to move his manufacturing facility to Dothan, Alabama.

This decision was a strategic move for transportation reasons. It was easier to move product to all points in the southeast from Dothan than from Tampa. A contract with Home Depot followed. Brad found himself and his crew working horrendous hours keeping up with orders. Waterfall Creation's business was booming and Brad was living his dream.

But in 2003 Brad ran head-on into another major challenge. This time it was a health issue. He contracted what the doctors eventually felt was Lyme disease. However, none of the many doctors he saw ever gave Brad a firm diagnosis or the definite cause of his illness.

As Brad's condition deteriorated, he got to the point that he could not carry on a conversation. Then, in New York State, he finally found a doctor who began a series of aggressive treatments for Lyme disease. Much of the medication used to eradicate the disease was found on the black market. It was powerful enough to kill him, but he felt that he needed to risk death in order to have a chance to live.

And live he did. Brad sold the company to concentrate on his health. It was a long road to recovery, but today Brad is a highly active person. He works at his leisure buying and repairing homes and is a very good tennis player.

Brad Vegas is a good illustration of how having something better begins with merely visualizing something better. Again, when we habitually visualize the life experiences we would like to see develop, that is the direction in which our efforts are most likely to carry us.

Life-Enhancement Message

Look up to soar high, for you will rarely rise above the level of your vision. What you clearly visualize is what you tend to work toward.

FIRST TWO LETTERS OF GOAL: GO

"A goal is developed from a vision about where we would like to be at some point in the future."—Dr. Wayne Dyer

With a great vision and a crystal-clear purpose embedded in our psyche, we are better prepared to revisit goals. Age has little to do with the practicality of rethinking life goals.

As I stated earlier, very few of us, early in our lives, knew with unshaken conviction and assurance what we wanted to do. I knew as a teenager that I wanted to be a professional baseball player. But wanting to be a pro and becoming a pro are two entirely different things. I did have the opportunity to play pro baseball for nine baseball seasons. What I had not given much thought and consideration to was what I would do after my baseball career ended. To enjoy any measure of success in life, it is crucial that we have a fairly accurate picture of what we intend to be after a series of life experiences.

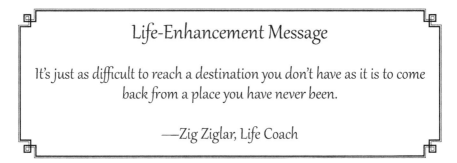

Life-Enhancement Message

It's just as difficult to reach a destination you don't have as it is to come back from a place you have never been.

—Zig Ziglar, Life Coach

GOT GOALS?

If I have learned anything over these years, the thing that counts the most is not where we stand, but in what direction we are moving. The old mountaineer reminds us, "Up heah in these heah mountains, you'd better know where you're goin' 'fore ya starts out, or ya gonna end up some place ya don't want to be."

If I were to ask you right now what your goals are, how would you respond? If you are like 95 percent of the people around you, your response will be something like this: *My goals are to be successful, to be happy, to make a lot of money, to enjoy a sense of security, to have a wonderful home life . . .*

While responses of this kind are common, there is an inherent problem with them: the answers do not set up the proper thought pattern to reach these goals. The reason is simple: it is because success, happiness, money, and security are the things we experience as we achieve specific goals that we aspire to reach. These are the by-product of reaching the goals we have envisioned.

Goals are easy to set in athletics. Goals are not, however, as easy to get a handle on in regular life. But shouldn't our goals extend far beyond work and career? I like to think that goals for all aspects of life, including personal matters, are good *for* us and good *to* us.

Nothing will have a greater impact on bringing direction to your career and life than will well-thought-out goals. Goals will be critical to all you want to accomplish in life. Consequently, one of the most important actions you can ever undertake is the process of goal setting.

Life-Enhancement Message

In the big scheme of things, what you obtain once reaching a goal is not as valuable as what you become by achieving the goal.

GOAL-SETTING KEYS

Think of setting goals in terms of planning a trip. First, you locate where you are. Then you decide where you want to go. Next you plan the route that will get you there. You also decide what you must bring with you to make the journey the best it possibly can be.

Part of your potential is found in how much time and effort you apply to answer these questions: Unless you know where you are going, how do you know when you have arrived? Unless you have legitimate goals for getting the results you want, what are the chances of obtaining the results you want? If you don't know what you need to help you along the way, how can you expect to actually get there?

Take it a step farther. Where do you want to be after having gone through a series of experiences? A clear picture of where you are and who you are is necessary if your life experiences are to be organized for establishing goals and achieving them.

I have discovered that, unless we have solid goals, it is virtually impossible to put our hearts and souls into our efforts. We tend to lack the extra energy and enthusiasm that gives specific directions to our endeavors, especially when confronted with obstacles and pushbacks.

Now, here comes the key question: Do you regularly set goals? Can you pull up in a moment's notice specifically stated goals in writing? Can you truly say what you want to achieve today or five years from now? The following ideas will help:

- Look backward as a means of deciding how to move forward. Goal setting is done from the future back to the present. The key is to learn from the past, plan for the future, and perform in the present.

- Set realistic and challenging daily, weekly, and seasonal goals that are desirable, believable, and achievable.

- Aim high enough to stretch yourself, but not so high that you never achieve what you set out to accomplish. Goals that are just out of reach, not completely out of sight, have the best motivational value.

- To be effective, goals must be measured by quantity, quality, and time. Otherwise, they are not worth the time spent on them.

- Write your goals down so you can see them, study them, and refer back to them. This gives you a chance to check up occasionally to determine the extent of your progress.

- Once you decide what your goals are, the next crucial step is to establish a pattern of how to achieve them. For goals to be reached, they have to harmonize with action.

- What obstacles, problems, and hurdles will stand between you and your goals? Determine what you might have to overcome to reach your goals. Then establish a plan that will push you right through these roadblocks.

- Share your goals with those who can encourage you, as well as help you in achieving them. Telling others what you want to achieve gets them involved and also reaffirms a commitment to yourself. Verbal affirmations are an excellent way to emphasize your visions.

- Set a deadline for each goal. Some goals may have natural dead-lines—length of time, etc.—but if they don't, set a deadline. Without time deadlines, goals are limited in value.

- If you don't have goals for achieving more than you have been achieving, the odds are good that you are achieving about as good as you are going to achieve.

Life-Enhancement Message

Dreams, desires, goals, and aspirations are all born in the heart and mind, and only there can they perish.

THE LONG-SHORT OF GOALS

A final thought on the goal issue is that it is wise for us to think in terms of establishing both long-term and short-term goals. Determining long-term goals several years out is simple. It is not easy, but it is sim-ple. It involves taking a real, hard look at who we are and what we can best do with the talents we have. This gives us a better perspective of what meaningful and significant long-range goals we can attain.

In reality, long-term goals are a commitment to our established purpose. Unless we have a consuming desire to achieve our pur-pose, it is virtually impossible to put a heart-and-soul effort into our daily affairs.

Long-term goals are designed to help keep us consistently on course. But it is the short-term goals that carry us up the success ladder, one rung at a time.

At the core of short-term goals is the principle of competition. Whatever our ultimate goals are, reaching these goals means we are in constant competition with our previous performance level as well as our future goals.

Why compete with ourselves? you might ask. When we are in competition with ourselves, it provides the self-motivation we need to keep aspiring to higher and higher levels. Our number one goal is to always work harder on improving ourselves than on anything else we do. Don't worry about trying to get ahead of others. The thrust behind your goals is to stay ahead of your prior performance level and elevate yourself so you are consistently rising higher.

Life-Enhancement Message

Possess an attitude of curiosity that enables you to tackle the future with a mentality of "What's next? Bring it on."

FOURTEEN

SUCCESS FORMS AROUND PREPARATION

The will to win matters; but in the scheme of things,
the will to prepare to win matters much more.
—Paul (Bear) Bryant, HOF Coach, University of Alabama

> You must be willing to prepare at a level you have never prepared at before if you expect to perform at a level you have never performed at before. In essence, to experience something new, you have to be willing to do something new.

THE WILL TO PREPARE TO WIN

There is probably little difference between your dreams and aspirations and those of almost anyone you know. All want to do well, to achieve something of significance, to be proud of themselves, to enjoy a great degree of financial success.

Wherein lies the difference in results obtained?

The most common cause of the lack of successful results is the absence of an aggressive will to win. But the will to win will be a frustrated desire unless there is an ever-present will to prepare to win.

The will to prepare to win is the little difference that makes the big difference in converting dreams and desires into reality. Winning is in proper preparation.

My recommendation is very plain: Create a mental picture of what a better future would look like, feel like, be like. From this base, you are in a good position to develop a plan that will prepare you for something better.

PREPARATION MOVES THE NEEDLE

Why is it that the top performers always make things look easy? Is it because they have more talent and ability than the rest of us? I believe the reason that top performers make things look effortless is because they have developed and perfected their mental and physical skills through preparation. They employ a deliberate and disciplined program of preparation to make themselves great.

There is a world of difference between having the tools to do something and using those tools to get things done. Every facet of our daily tasks and chores depends on the degree of the preparation we make for performing them. Our best abilities can only be fully recognized and utilized when we lay the ground work for them to flourish. If we passionately possess the determination to properly prepare, the odds of succeeding are definitely in our favor. It is a required custom of anyone desiring to be a top performer.

Those who have experienced great things were not great from the start, but they realized the importance of developing a superior program of preparation. They were aware that they could only do well in what they were well equipped to do. No more. No less. If there is one lesson I can pass along to those reaching for more, it is to stress the importance of thorough preparation. It is easy to talk about how we are going to prepare better in the future, but we fail to realize that a little of the future arrives each day.

In sports, the successful athletic teams do not become successful on the day of a game. They become successful on the lengthy days of training prior to game day. My friend Coach Sonny Smith, who spent over thirty years as a collegiate basketball coach, is quoted as saying, "Preparation puts brains in your muscles." For us the reverse may be true: Preparation puts muscles in our brains.

The most common cause of a lack of quality results is the absence of an aggressive will to prepare to succeed. Performing at a higher level is dependent on just how badly we are willing to raise our level of readiness. Even the outcome of our daily tasks and chores depends on the degree of the preparation we make for performing them.

Let me emphasize just how critical it is to have a plan in place before we begin to execute any effort toward attaining something great. I am talking about being prepared inside and out, up and down, backward and forward, to do what it takes to achieve at every task you face. Ask yourself, *Am I totally ready to work toward being the very best I can possibly be?* Unmet expectations become the norm if knowledge and understanding lack the substance and direction that comes from developing quality preparation habits.

In sports, we use the term "preparation drips with perspiration." Another way we can look at it is, "Life preparation drips of inspiration." Are you inspired to prepare to be your best?

PREPARATION HABITS

Almost everyone wants to be highly successful until they understand what it takes to be highly successful. Until there is a perception that preparation habits are crucial to success, how successful can any of us be? To sit back hoping that a little action here or there will be the magic pill that leads to quality results is the epitome of disappointment. To change reality, change perception.

Successful results are triggered by a rush of deliberate and continuous action in the preparation phase of what you do. Listen to these words of a very successful football coach, Nick Saban: "Winning is a lot of hard work and preparation. You can't be complacent. . . . [You] must learn what you are supposed to do and be able to go out there and do it on a consistent basis."

I probably have said this somewhere before: you cannot become the person you want to be unless you are willing to do something that you have never consistently done before. To say it another way, whatever got you where you are today won't be good enough to keep you there tomorrow. Every facet of your daily activities depends on the degree of the preparation you are routinely making for performing them better and better.

One of the most important things you can do for yourself is to pause a moment and ask yourself, *What do I need to be doing right now to become the person that I believe I can become?*

Be straight up with yourself. With your present experience and current skill set, what preparation habits do you need to improve to put you on the road to greater results? Are you ready to spend your time and energy preparing to extend beyond what you are? It is from this reality base that you can move confidently forward in making the statement "You can be anything you want to be" a truism.

File these thoughts away somewhere in your mental computer:

- Preparation may not always bring success, but there is no success without preparation.

- It is not preparing for the things you *like* to do that will make you more successful. It is preparing for the things you *must* do to be successful.

- The fundamental theme behind your preparation efforts should be to move beyond what you are for the greater achievement of what you can become.

- A priceless performance of anything always will be preceded by paying the price at preparing for a priceless performance.

- Performing up to the very best level during every sales opportunity is less a question of what you desire as it is a question of what you are willing to do to prepare to perform at that level.

- Preparation only makes a difference when your preparation is the right kind of preparation. To put it another way: Preparation does not make perfect; perfect preparation makes perfect.

Life-Enhancement Message

Prepare to do the things you are expected to do when you are expected to do them so when it is time for the actual performance, you will do the things you are expected to in the way that you are expected to do them.

—Leonard Bernstein

IMPROVING PREPARATION HABITS

Two habits you must strive to eliminate—

- The habit of placing limits on yourself
- The habit of letting others place limits on you

The three stages of habits—

1. Stranger

2. Companion

3. Master (good or bad?)

A great way to improve your preparation habits is to

- seek the advice you need to have, not the advice you would like to hear; and
- be willing to attach yourself to those who know what you need to know.

"You will never perform any better than your preparation habits allow you to perform."—Paul (Bear) Bryant

CLEANING OUT OLD HABITS

An important part of preparation is cleaning out old habits to make room for new ones. Listen to these words:

> My name is Habit. I am something that you created because of continual and similar behavior. I am your constant companion and closest friend. Show me exactly how you want something done, and after a very short time, I will do it without your willful assent. Most of the tasks you do will eventually become mine because I am able to do them without question or hesitation. I am one of your greatest assets, provided you have trained me properly. But if you have not prepared me properly, my actions will rob you of the opportunity to be better and different. That you can rest assured will be the case.
>
> —Author Unknown

Because old habits are so deeply ingrained, they are usually hard to reverse. But it is also important to remember that we are ultimately responsible for our habits. In the beginning, we make our habits, but in the end, our habits make us. A key factor in learning how to change automatic defensive reactions that have become habits is being consciously aware of them. Until we acknowledge how they affect our lives, we will continue to react to our surroundings with old, antiquated behavior.

Once self-awareness is in place, we need to have the patience to learn a new habit. It will take about three weeks before we begin to see the results of our new actions. Frustration can emerge in the beginning of learning a new behavior pattern. But remember, each day change becomes easier, and before long, we have replaced an old habit with a better one.

Life-Enhancement Message

It takes little effort to prepare to dance in fair weather, but it takes exceptional preparation to prepare for the storm. Then, when bad weather comes, we don't have to wait for the storm to pass; we have learned to dance in the rain.

THE STANDARD: DO YOUR BEST

We will never perform any better than our preparation habits allow us to perform. There is nothing we do that good habits of preparation cannot help us do better. Quality habits help us establish a standard around which we conduct our daily activities: they lead us on a path of doing our best day in and day out. Developing winning work habits is something that begins inside of us, not around us. Do you have a standard for your work habits that encourages your best? Personal standards are the only standards that hold up on a daily basis.

It is while we are actively engaged in the work process that our best ideas arise. If we are sitting around trying to dream up great ideas, we can sit there a long time before anything comes to us. But if we are in the process of work, an idea will pop into our minds. Then something else may come up, and then something else that might push us in another, more positive direction. The key to generating ideas is found in the work process, where we get into a flow of action and thought which will make good things happen.

When your preparation habits lead you on a path of doing your best, you have a good chance of ending up performing with excellence. You have laid the groundwork in order to do so. Set the bar high, but always remember that excellence will be good enough.

Mental Preparation Schedule

I will not let yesterday's performance affect today's effort.
I will make my biggest goal today one that outdoes yesterday.
I will do something today that I have only thought about doing.

I will perform today in such a way that tomorrow will be better.

I will perform what is expected of me today—and then some.

I will not concern myself with tomorrow today until today becomes tomorrow.

FIFTEEN

UNBLOCK YOUR BLOCK

To laugh is to risk appearing the fool.
To weep is to risk appearing sentimental.
To reach out to another is to risk involvement.
To expose feelings is to risk exposing your
*   true self.*
To place your ideas and dreams before a crowd is
*   to risk their loss.*
To love is to risk not being loved in return.
To live righteously is to risk ridicule.
To hope is to risk despair. To try is to risk failure.
But risk must be taken because the greatest hazard
*   in life is to risk nothing.*
Those who risk nothing do little, have little, and
*   generally end up with little.*
Chained by their certitude to safekeeping, they
*   forfeit their freedom.*
Only a person who risks is free.

—Adapted from an unknown source

There is one thing I can promise will happen in this chapter: I will be redundant. I am going to repeat the same message numerous times, using different wording as we go, because what I want to leave with you is that important. I want you to think about what happens when you "unblock your block." I want you to grab hold of the concept that success involves an element of risk. Generally, the higher the risk the greater the potential for big rewards.

RISK:REWARD

"Life ultimately rewards creativity and innovation."—Tony Robbins

We are all limited to the extent that we can satisfy our dreams and desires by our talents, abilities, and resources. But the most influential limit is not what we are, but rather what we decide to do with what we are. The course we follow in taking what we have and making it better is influenced by the types of risks we are willing to take.

A high level of success requires a higher level of risk. Too many of us let fear limit our ability to stare risk in the eye. We let the desire to play it safe reduce our expectations and our will to be proactive. Over time we shift to a lower gear and find ourselves taking what is left over by those who are willing to act and act big.

To succeed in an extraordinary way calls for the continuous process of making risk-to-reward decisions. Creating thoughtful risk-to-reward decisions is a crucial aspect of becoming a top-notch performer at anything.

One of the greatest success stories of all time is Sam Walton. He started his business career at J.C. Penney in 1945. Later on, he and his brother Bud owned fifteen Ben Franklin Variety Stores.

In 1962, Sam broke away to start Wal-Mart in a small town in Arkansas. There were no bright lights or big-city glitz for Walton. Wal-Mart became the darling of small-town USA.

I had a chance meeting with Mr. Walton back in the late '70s. I had forgotten my toothbrush and asked the hotel clerk for the nearest place I could buy one. He pointed me toward a new store that was opening in town called Wal-Mart.

I was greeted at the door by a middle-aged gentleman. As usual, my inquisitive mind wanted to know more about Wal-Mart since I had never heard of the store. He graciously answered a couple of my questions and told me where I would find a toothbrush. On the way out, there was another gentleman at the door greeting people.

I inquired about the previous gentlemen who had greeted me. "Oh, you are talking about Mr. Walton. He is the owner," the greeter offered while nodding his head.

"Nice gentleman," I said. Wished I had talked to Mr. Walton in more detail.

By the year 2010, Wal-Mart had become the largest corporation in the world. Sam Walton demonstrated many vital lessons on how to succeed, but none more important than to have a game plan and the courage to fail. Walton's success entailed risk, but he understood that's what it would take to enjoy the rewards.

Risk and opportunity are two sides of the same coin. In every opportunity there is risk. But it is equally true that in every risk there is the possibility of a great opportunity.

> Few things in life limit us as much as the attitude of playing it safe. A safe place is not necessarily a secure place. The only safe place is never where we are right now. It's up ahead. And when we think we have arrived at a safe destination, we will find that's even farther up the road.

RISK OPPORTUNITY

Why is it when it comes time to step up and take a measured risk opportunity, the courage to do so is often missing? Why is it when we're right on the brink of something promising materializing, talented people back off and fail to engage the risk-to-reward relationship?

One of the biggest encumbrances in risk-management decisions is the tendency to want all of the possible roadblocks to be overcome before taking action. We want to feel safe before making a decision that involves an element of risk. The future of any risk opportunity is always uncertain. There are no guarantees. No doubt, the willingness to take more risks increases the odds of more setbacks. Some of the risks we take are bound to turn out unfavorably. It is indeed rare to enjoy uninterrupted success without times of disappointment. But with limited risk comes the guarantee for lower prospects of possible rewards, as well.

If we are not big enough to go for it, we will rarely be big enough to succeed. In other words, if we are afraid of failing at anything, we shift the odds in favor of failing. Exposing ourselves to failure is the price we must pay in order to present ourselves to success. Taking more prudent risks makes the future brighter by enriching the opportunities available to us. The odds of success become more certain when we have the mental fortitude to measure the risk-to-reward ratio and then proceed with deliberate action.

Branch Rickey knew something about taking risks. Those of you who are baseball purists will recognize his name. Mr. Rickey has been referred to as "the Monarch of Modern Baseball."

Mr. Rickey was a special consultant for the St. Louis Cardinals during my first year in spring training camp, in 1961. Players would sit in the midst of palm trees to listen to him talk baseball. He called it "holding court."

A quote of Mr. Rickey's that I have carried with me through the years is, "Luck is the product of design." Another quote that stuck with me is, "The most successful way to succeed is to stick your neck out." Mr. Rickey really stuck his neck out to bring an end to segregation in baseball. It was his decision to bring Jackie Robinson to the Brooklyn Dodgers in 1947. Robinson was the first black player to play in the modern era of the major leagues. It was a risk of the first order, but Mr. Rickey had done his homework on Robinson. He saw Jackie as a person who was educated and had impeccable character and unquestionable talent. But above these things, Mr. Rickey felt Robinson could handle the chaos and turmoil that would surround his presence on and off the field. He felt Jackie had a strong sense of diplomacy. And he was right.

Mr. Rickey was also the individual credited with creating the framework for the modern minor-league baseball farm system, as well as signing Roberto Clemente, the first Hispanic superstar. He also introduced the batting helmet to major league baseball.

Taking measured risks is the price we must pay for making progress. Those who are afraid to take these kinds of risks may avoid the pain that comes to those who attempt something and fail. But they also forfeit the deep-felt sense of well-being that comes to those who change, grow, and make progress toward enjoying a better life.

PROGRESS IS OUT FRONT

A law of life reads, "You either progress or regress, you don't stand still." To make progress, we must step out of our sheltered world and venture beyond the familiar to engage the unknown. Progress indicates we go where we have never gone. The path is always in front of us. Progress is built around the belief that there is always a greater experience going forward. And there always is. The experience in itself is invaluable.

My friend John Leonard is a great example of what I am talking about. John had been an executive in the shipyard and shipbuilding business for twenty-nine years when he left his job in 2003. After a year of working as a consultant, John was unemployed and watching TV at home when the telephone rang. It was a former associate on the other end with a potential business opportunity. As John would say, "I was doing nothing when I get a call that offered me an opportunity to become a part of a new company." The company founders had found a niche that they could fill in the offshore-drilling segment of the oil-production industry. John said yes, and joined the company as a partner in January of 2005. The company needed John's organizational skills and business experience. It may have been a measured risk on John's part, but a risk well worth taking.

After four years of great success, a much larger company made an offer to buy a portion of the business from John and his partners. The larger company wanted a presence in the offshore-oil-drilling business to enhance the value of one of its existing businesses. John and his partners sold that part of the business in 2008, but their LLC also owned a subsidiary company that the buyer did not want. John and his partners were able to keep the subsidiary company, and that has worked out to be a bonanza, as well.

While sitting at home wondering what he was going to do next to reach a position of financial security, John dared to dive into uncertainty. He said yes to a risk opportunity, and the rest is history.

Each one of us needs to ask ourselves, *Am I giving progress a chance to happen?* The greatest hazard we face in life is the failure to engage life to the fullest and give ourselves an opportunity to spend life living.

It is a damaging roadblock to progress when we sit back and wait for something to happen, rather than attempt to make something happen. "Nothing ventured, nothing gained" is as true today as the day it was first spoken. We can either have life lead us or we can lead ourselves to the life we want.

How have you been doing in the progress-making arena? Are you willing to accept quality risk management as a way of life? The odds of making progress will be in your favor when taking quality risks is your trademark.

WHERE ARE THE OPPORTUNITIES?

"Unblock your block" has at its core the premise that neither you nor I wish to be blinded by certitude, nor a slave to mediocrity. It carries a greater meaning in the desire to look for life-enhancing opportunities. I have observed that opportunities tend to look better going than they do coming. This is true for those who let "ifs" and "buts" become their hallmark.

Please understand that just because something appears impossible, it doesn't necessarily lessen the chance of it being an opportunity. There is always someone around who gobbles up the opportunities that have been left on the table by others. It is wise to keep in mind that opportunities wait for no one. A lifetime opportunity must be experienced in the lifetime of that opportunity.

What is the best way to take advantage of the opportunities we have available to us? I can guarantee you that it seldom depends on being at the right place at the right time. It depends on being ready at any time. Look at it this way: The only opportunity that will personally ever count is the one you and I are willing to pursue. What we might consider to be no opportunity may well turn out to be our best opportunity.

Opportunities come in many forms. They are found in unusual places. They come from all sorts of directions, but they only come when we are facing forward and toward the future, not backward and toward the past.

What opportunity lies before you, right now? Are you ready to grasp it? Nourish it? Cherish it? Make the most of it?

You can never look for an opportunity too soon because you never know when it will be too late. The hour of opportunity is always now.

FEAR OF FAILING

I am convinced that the main reason we fail to act on promising opportunities is that we fear we will fail. No one can fail at something unless they make an effort, can they? They cannot succeed at anything without the possibility of failing, either.

We all have the willingness inside of us to complete a task once we start it. This drive propels us forward. It's the reason many simply forego an attempt, knowing that it would set in motion momentum toward the unknown. To save face, some would rather run the risk of missing out on a prime opportunity that could impact their lives in a positive way than to confront the possibility that they might not like themselves or the outcome if they have little, or no, success. It is not uncommon to find those among us who would rather refrain from running the risk of making something good happen than to face self-doubt and personally induced hurdles.

Nothing is more injurious to achievement than the lack of application. Many of us begin with great intentions but fail to put them into action. Although we talk about doing this or that, we end up doing little or nothing. It is not the lack of opportunities that creates our biggest problem, it is our inability to recognize them and then seize them.

I have said this before. Let me say it again: Isn't it far better to have the courage to act and attempt to make something happen than to fail to act and make nothing happen? At the very least, we have the satisfaction of knowing that we are making every effort to create something better for our lives. There are potential consequences when we do nothing, just as there are consequences when we attempt something and fail.

When we come up short, we have the satisfaction of knowing that we gave ourselves every chance to succeed. We took the risk to extend ourselves beyond our fears in anticipation of greater rewards.

In 1955, the American Family Life Assurance Company of Columbus, Georgia, was founded. It is the company we know today as AFLAC. The founding fathers were three brothers, John, Bill, and Paul Amos. Their grandfather Isaac Amos and my great-grandmother Rebeckah Amos were brother and sister.

The oldest of the three brothers, John, was a lawyer and a visionary. He is responsible for founding the company and providing its early vision.

Bill was the middle brother and known as the nuts-and-bolts operations guru. Bill knew how to keep company costs down even while the company was growing by leaps and bounds.

Paul was the salesman. He had a knack for creativity and introduced a unique selling idea that would change the scope of the company. Paul's son, Dan Amos, is presently at the helm of AFLAC, a job he has held for over two decades. Because of Dan, AFLAC has seen remarkable growth and profitability. He is responsible for having placed AFLAC into the position as a worldwide leader in the insurance industry and one of the top companies in the USA.

But things did not go well in the beginning for the Amos brothers. After struggling for three years selling life, health, and accident insurance door-to-door in Georgia and Alabama, the company was on the brink of failure. That's when John Amos decided that the company should enter the supplemental insurance business.

In 1958, AFLAC developed and introduced a supplementary cancer-expense insurance policy. By finding a specific marketing niche, the company turned the corner and began its ascendance toward being one of the top five hundred companies in America.

Two unique ideas were behind the tremendous growth. Through the creativity of Paul Amos, AFLAC pioneered a unique selling idea that clustered sales at worksites. AFLAC sales representatives went to companies and made sales pitches to groups of employees instead of to individuals. Today, almost 98 percent of AFLAC's United States policies are bought through payroll deductions.

The second unique idea, and the one that brought the company out of obscurity, was the introduction of the AFLAC duck in 1999. A worker for the company's New York ad firm was walking in Central Park in New York City when he noticed that the quack of a duck sounded very similar to "AFLAC." So was born the AFLAC duck, and, as the saying goes, the rest is history.

The Amos family had several great ideas that they relentlessly pursued to make AFLAC one of the elite companies in the world. They stared failure in the face and made success-producing decisions that changed the course of the company. Their success illustrates that if we engender the willingness to act and get into the flow of things, we won't think about not succeeding. Instead, all of our efforts will be focused on reaching beyond toward the greater rewards.

As retired General Jim Mattis once said, "Winners don't know how to spell defeat." It is important that we listen to the best part of us that places no limits on our ability to manage risks and come out on top.

What we should be thinking about are the chances we get to change our lives when we take reasonable risks. Isn't the best success policy one in which we have done everything possible to succeed?

DON'T STRIKE OUT LOOKING

When I was pitching baseballs for a living, I was not known as a "strikeout pitcher." Anything but that. On the rare occasions when I would record a strikeout, it would be of the "called third strike" variety, meaning the batter did not offer at a pitch that the umpire called for a third strikeout.

From the batter's perspective, there is an old baseball adage that says, "You cannot hit home runs unless you are willing to strike out." Something needs to be added to this: If you are going to strike out, do it swinging the bat. Don't leave the batter's box with the bat on your shoulder.

Nothing leads to a more miserable existence than being habitually indecisive when an important at-bat (decision) is at hand. We can never have it any different unless we are willing to consistently swing the bat. Indecision affects each of us at some point and in some way, just as it does the baseball hitter. The inability to make key, timely decisions not only mars the present, it dims the brightness of the future, as well. *I wish I had only* . . . is the hallmark of too many who failed to swing the bat in crucial life situations.

Check the records of Babe Ruth and Hank Aaron, two of Major League Baseball's all-time-best home run hitters. Rarely is it mentioned that the two of them were among the all-time leaders in strikeouts. Proof enough that to hit home runs we must be willing to strike out. Remember that every opportunity to be successful carries with it the seeds of failure. It also carries the chance to be highly successful. To perform in an extraordinary way, measurable risks must be taken.

Obviously, being capable of swinging the bat and making key decisions is a learned behavior. And, like any other habit, it can be developed. It becomes easier to take healthy cuts at the ball in life. We have the luxury in our daily activities of taking the time to weigh the evidence of what lies before us. A baseball hitter, on the other hand, must make quick decisions. Results are known immediately.

However, most of our decisions, notably those of a life-changing nature, should be made after careful thought and deliberation. We generally have time to weigh the possibilities and consequences before we decide to swing the bat or not.

How are you doing in this area of swinging the bat when faced with a major decision? Even if you do take a swing, the decision may not turn out the way you would like. There are no guarantees.

But isn't it far better to make the decision to swing the bat and have a chance to hit a home run than to fail to swing at all and go down with the regret of not trying?

IF I HAD ONLY . . .

It is important to remember that our strength always lies in the present. But what happens to us when we get out of the present? As I see it, hindrances to our capacity to function in the present arise on two fronts: rushing forward toward the future without being properly prepared, and stubbornly clinging to the past.

The first group fails to fully explore future options in light of their purposes and values. Because they do not take the time to examine where they are headed, they end up chasing what turns out to be little that can add to a promising future.

The second group attempts to hold on to the past. They want things to be like they were. As a result, they deprive themselves of the newness that is derived from a fresh vision and a new start.

Do you have a tendency to act in either of these directions? Here's the confession of an old friend, Buster Milner, who wrote these words many years ago:

"I stood at the front door of life and watched a long procession ease by. It was a parade of 'my yesterdays' that moved along before me.

I viewed my triumphs, my failures, the good moments, my bad moments, a stream of memories, and even a long line of missed opportunities. As the procession moved away from me, I found myself making one last grasp to grab hold of an opportunity that I had missed before.

But to no avail. As much as I wanted to relive something from yesterday, it strolled along into oblivion. It left me with nothing but today."

Sound familiar? It is easy to look back at yesterday and the days before that and say, *If I had only . . .* , isn't it? But where will this get us? We know that we can't go back in time. We know that we can't live our yesterdays again. But there is a tendency to still try, isn't there?

If there ever was a mental challenge that confronted us, it is in making peace with our past. Some of us have a tough time forgetting what has been before. We spend too much of the best days of our lives recycling yesterdays. We keep bringing up what might have been or what should have been. But the more we replay yesterday, the farther away we get from today's opportunities and the tougher it is to move forward.

It is important for us to understand that yesterday is always with us, leaving its legacy. For better or worse, it is scattered all over the road behind us. But those past experiences encompass wisdom and livable lessons that can be used and take root in life today. Where we come from and who we've been never leave us and will always be part of who we are today. The trick is to know what to take from that while we are heading toward the future. Yesterday may be a great place to visit, but it's a worthless place to live.

Life-Enhancement Message

You know what you have done. You know how far you have come. But if you don't know what you are capable of doing, you don't know how far you can go. The challenge before you every day is to keep expanding your horizons as if there are no limits to your potential. It is a challenge that you can meet when you are always striving to make prudent decisions today that will impact tomorrow.

OPENNESS TO NEW EXPERIENCES

There comes a time when we must push the reset button if we are to enjoy any measure of success in life. Is it time to rewind your risk-opportunity button? Are you up to the task?

Hopefully, the point has been made that we must take risks in order to make progress. It is also important that we seek the virtues of an openness to new experiences to keep us reaching and growing.

When we have an openness to new experiences, we are not imprisoned by comfortable habits. We are not trapped by routine. We do not cling to the familiar. We do not over seek security nor choose the path of least resistance. We face life with a staff in our hands instead of a crutch.

Beethoven, the great music composer, had a favorite maxim: "The barriers are not yet erected which can say to aspiring talent and industry, 'thus far and no farther.'"

"Thus far and no farther" is what happens to us when we seek security at any cost, when there is no openness to experience. Instead, we prefer to stick with doing things the same way, even when conditions reveal that we should be doing something else.

Let me ask you again: Has this area of taking risks been a challenge for you? If it has been, I sense that you are ready to move beyond the status quo. You are ready to stretch yourself and extend your capabilities. You are ready to do the things you never imagined you could do. You are ready to experience results that you have never experienced before.

Store these words of Darwin P. Kingsley away somewhere in your mental computer: "There are no limitations in what you can do except the limitations in your own mind as to what you cannot do."

SIXTEEN

FUEL YOUR STAYING POWER

You have certainly suffered many setbacks in your life: Did you not fall down the first time you stood and tried to walk? You felt like you were going to drown the first time you tried to swim, didn't you? Did you ride a bicycle the first time you sat on the seat and tried to pedal? You missed hitting the ball the first time you swung the bat, right? Did you have a correct answer for that math equation the first time you tried to solve it?

Some of the greatest retailers in this country experienced numerous failures before finding their underpinnings that led to success. R. H. Macy failed seven times before his store in New York became a success. J. C. Penney opened his first store, The Golden Rule Store, in a small Wyoming town in 1902, but it took him years to get the J.C. Penney stores off the ground. He was still active in the business well into his nineties. F. W. Woolworth was told his five-and-dime Woolworth concept would never succeed, and his first one did fail. Yet he went on to become one of the greatest retailers of all time.

The history book of business is full of people who had every reason to throw up their hands and walk away but didn't. When we are working hard and being aggressive to advance our careers, making mistakes will be a given for most of us. We are going to do the wrong thing at times. If we are not making mistakes along the way, then we are not doing enough to enjoy any greater measure of success. Some potholes are inevitable on the road to success.

Yogi Berra is quoted as saying, "You are what you are when the going gets tough." Former pro football great Alex Karras reminds us, "Toughness is in your soul and spirit, not in your muscles."

Life-Enhancement Message

Sometimes you get knocked off your feet by something beyond your control. But when you get knocked down by something or someone, the responsibility still falls to you to get up. Just remember: no one is ever a failure by getting knocked down; they only become a failure if they don't get back up and then do their best to stay up!

FLAWED BUT KICKIN'

Why is it that we spend considerable time and energy trying to avoid the possibility of making mistakes? To keep our hold on reality, we have to grasp the fact that mistakes have happened and will continue to happen. That's a part of life. That's a part of growth.

Those who attempt to avoid making errors generally are passed up by those who are not afraid to make them. If you are a major league baseball fan, you understand that a batter who has a lifetime batting average of .300 is Hall of Fame material. Think about that: a batter who is only successful three out of ten times at bat is considered a rousing success. The one great lesson from this scenario is the manner in which the better baseball hitters handle the failure of not getting a hit. They recognize that the key to their success doesn't lie in the misses, it lies in their ability to be consistent in their approach and not let their 70 percent failure affect their 30 percent success.

One of the most useless ways to spend our time is trying to be perfect in an imperfect world. It is just not going to happen. Like the baseball hitter, we have to learn to live with setbacks along the way. "Flawed but kickin'" is a fairly good description of those who are striving for perfection but settle for excellence. They know that perfection exists in rare air.

An associate of Thomas Edison, the master inventor of the lightbulb and other incredible innovations, once asked him, "Sir, do you realize we have made fifty thousand mistakes?" Edison calmly replied, "No, what we've done is found fifty thousand things that won't work."

I wonder how many times you and I have been told to learn from our mistakes. Think about it a moment: What are we going to learn? Like Thomas Edison, we will learn the things that don't work, right? Success in many endeavors grows out of a process of elimination.

On one of the minor league teams I played for, I had a manager who was a former batting instructor at the major league level. Our team was taking batting practice prior to a game against the hardest throwing pitcher on the team's roster. Most of the hitters were having little success hitting the ball. The manager grabbed a bat and said to the hitters standing around the batting cage, "Let me show ya boys something." After swinging and missing three pitches, he turned to the hitters and said, "Now ya boys see what ya doin' wrong."

Let me emphasize again that uninterrupted success is indeed rare. The complexity of living a forward-looking life is too great not to expect some mistakes along the way. We must have the courage to accept an occasional mistake as the price of progress. Rest assured that if we are afraid of making a mistake, at some point we will make a mistake.

Being willing to do things wrong offers a learning laboratory to discover what is right. It's not the mistake that makes us doubt ourselves, but the wrong perception of the value of the mistake. Every time we stumble, we have an opportunity to learn something. A mistake should not be in vain. It offers us very important lessons that we can use going forward. It is crucial that we not lose the value of the lessons.

When a mistake is made and then corrected, it is an opportunity to improve and make progress. The eraser on a pencil is not there to correct mistakes, it is there for those who are willing to correct their mistakes. Lessons are learned that wouldn't have existed without the opportunity to live through them.

If we are not making some mistakes along the way, it is a reflection that we are not trying our best to move ahead. It means we are being too cautious. It was Tom Peters, the noted author, who said, "If it is worth doing, it is worth doing wrong."

We will have the opportunity to correct many mistakes along our career path. To do so, though, we have to cultivate a workable relationship with our miscalculations. We must see our mistakes as friends who can bring great benefits for learning.

Other thoughts to ponder about mistakes:

- To admit you made a mistake is a sign of strength, not a display of weakness.

- A mistake does not define you; the next opportunity does.

- Mistakes are reasons for growth, not excuses for quitting.

- You can rest assured that if you are afraid of making a mistake, at some point you will make a mistake.

- To never admit making mistakes enhances the chances of making them again.

- An eraser is not for those who make mistakes, it is for those willing to correct their mistakes.

- Learn from the mistakes of others. Your career will not be long enough to make them all yourself.

- It's amazing how there's never enough time to do it right the first time, but there is always time to do it over.

- Just think about how much trouble you might have spared yourself if you could have had your second chance first.

- It was Benjamin Franklin who said, "Those things that hurt instruct." Each mistake we make is an instructor ready to assist our growth.

SEE ME THROUGH

The only attribute that wears well and holds its color through thick and thin is staying power. It is cut from the fabric of persistence and woven with perseverance. No areas in life are immune to this combination. We can only go as far as our staying power will allow us.

As I mentioned in an early chapter, I am a history buff. One of my favorite historical people is Abraham Lincoln. I find his background to be full of life messages. During the Civil War, President Lincoln was noted for visiting the wounded soldiers at several hospitals in the Washington area. On one hospital visit, he came to the bed of a young soldier barely hanging on to life. The president was stirred to stop and visit for a few minutes. He took a seat close to the young soldier's bed. The dying man did not recognize Lincoln. He asked the very busy president if he would write his mother a letter. President Lincoln proceeded to write down the words offered by the young soldier. After finishing the letter, the president inquired if there was anything else he could do.

"Yes, sir, I don't think I'm gonna last much longer. Would you please see me through?"

Lincoln moved closer to the young man and wrapped his long arms around him. The very overburdened president knew the value of supporting this young, dying soldier, and he did it the best he knew how. For hours, Lincoln held the young man close to his chest, until the young soldier drew his final breath. The president had taken the time to see the young man through.

If there ever was an individual who knew something about seeing things through, it was Lincoln. Think about how many times he faced defeat and adversity, but he hung in there and saw things through. Look at this track record. Before becoming the president of the United States, Abraham Lincoln

> was defeated for the state legislature,
> was a failure in business,
> was defeated for Speaker of the House,
> was defeated for Congress,
> was defeated for the US Senate,
> was defeated for nomination as vice president,
> was defeated again for the US Senate, and
> then was elected president of the United States.

President Lincoln's political life teaches us a great lesson about how to handle the lack of immediate success. This is the kind of lesson that can be a driving force to help us refine and strengthen our efforts going forward. Remember Lincoln.

See It Through

When you are up against a tough foe,
Meet it squarely, face-to-face;
Lift your chin and set your shoulders,
Plant your feet and secure your place.
You really don't want to try to dodge it,
Just do the best you can do;
You may fail—then again, you may not—
But you won't know until you
See it through!

Even if all you do appears to no avail,
And the outcome looks very grim,
Don't let your determination desert you;
Keep your vigor and vim.
For if the worst is bound to happen,
In spite of all that you can do,
Running from it will not save you;
So hang in there and
See it through!

Your best effort may often seem futile
And give you reasons to fret;
But just keep in mind you are facing
What all successful people once met.
If you have to fail, go down fighting;
Don't give up whatever you do;
Chin up and head high to the finish;
Who knows what might happen
When you **see it through!**

—Author Unknown

TRY, TRY AGAIN

Do you remember the maxim we heard as kids "If at first you don't succeed, try, try again"? It still applies.

The one great lesson I learned as a baseball pitcher was when you surrender a home run, you best get over it quickly and move on to the next batter. There is an element of immediacy in being a baseball pitcher. The results of a pitch are instant. This is generally not the case out in the real world.

We may not know the results of our efforts for some time. Then, when we do get the results, they may not be to our liking. The one thing that sets high achievers apart from the crowd is they use setbacks to do their best growing. As my uncle Louie would say, "There's always more fertilizer in the valley than on the mountain."

Most successful people are among the most resilient people on earth. They have a supportive feeling that, even when they give their best effort and come up short, gives them more determination to seek the next challenge.

High achievers understand that the more attempts they make, the more chances they have to be successful. By acting on what they have learned, they broaden their capacity for moving the needle much farther toward the side of success.

Life-Enhancement Message

Your decision to hang in there beyond what you think
is your threshold brings you in touch with an otherwise
unknown inner confidence. This will help you bridge the gap
from failure to success, and from losing to winning.

IT AIN'T OVER 'TIL IT'S OVER

One of the favorite clichés of sportscasters is the old Yogi Berra saying, "It ain't over 'til it's over."

It is easy to jump to the conclusion that something is over when things look bleak. Yet an essential part of developing a champion's mentality is to hang in there when the going gets tough and success appears out of sight. It's not easy to enthusiastically do our best when quality results appear out of reach, and having moments of doubt and thoughts of buckling is understandable. To actually give in, however, is a harmful reaction to a temporary emotion.

It is important that we never, never give in deep down on the inside. One of the greatest speeches of all time was seven words long. It was rendered by Prime Minister Winston Churchill of Great Britain, who said, "Never, never, never, never, never give up!"

Quitting is not an option so long as there is still hope. It takes grit to hold our ground when succeeding is in grave doubt. Again, the words of Yogi Berra ring sound and true: "It ain't over 'til it's over!" Grit calls for one of the most demanding forms of mental discipline required of any achiever. It is the choice to stay in there and hold our resolve when our best efforts appear futile. Even if the odds are stacked against us, when we stay the course we arrive at a better situation than before.

Life-Enhancement Message

There is no defeat except within, and unless you are defeated there, you'll always find a way to win.
—Author Unknown

Bill Bussey has been a long-time friend of mine. Most folks know Bill as "Bubba." He is co-host, with Rick Burgess, of the nationally syndicated *Rick & Bubba Show*, a show that has been around for a quarter of a century. Rick and Bubba were the first to host a radio interview of a new president of the USA named Donald Trump.

Bill developed a passion for radio broadcasting prior to his teen years. His trip from a kid wanting to be behind a radio mike to actually getting there took him years. Let's examine the trip Bill took in search of realizing a dream and a goal. The radio learning curve for Bill was honed on the campus of Jacksonville State University, in Jacksonville, Alabama. He became a fixture around 92J, the college radio station.

Bill and Rick met in a Spanish class at Jacksonville State. They both worked at the college radio station. Rick was an on-air person. Bill served as the station's engineer and was involved in promotions. What was missing for Bill was the cherished job of being an on-air talent.

The challenges for Bill were constantly changing. Fast forward a few years. Bill was serving as chief engineer for a couple of stations in Gadsden, Alabama, when he was asked by the management of Q104 to recruit Rick to host a morning show. Rick was doing a morning show in Oxford, Alabama. Rick accepted the offer from Q104. When Rick came over to Q104, he and Bill started hanging out at lunch. Soon Bill was doing a part-time gig on the morning show. But Bill's goal of being a full-time, on-air personality was thwarted by the station's general manager, who felt Bill had a lingering and fatal flaw for radio: the way he spoke. Bill had what we refer to in the South as a country accent. The feeling was that Bill's accent wouldn't play, not even in Gadsden, Alabama.

The realization that his career as an on-air personality had been put on hold just made Bill that much more determined. He remained steadfast in his desire to be a broadcaster. One day, Rick asked Bill to recite some passages from Shakespeare. It was both a hoot and a hit. Bill sounded like a real "Bubba" to many. And Bubba he became.

The station's general manager, who previously would not allow Bill to be on the air, started singing a new tune. Soon the Rick & Bubba Show was off and running. Their kinship and chemistry began to grow.

Bill Bussey had a new name, Bubba, and a new opportunity to realize a long-sought goal. He proved that the future is often beholden to those who see the future as a means of achieving in the here and now. He demonstrated that every day "we can."

"No matter what you do, sometimes things don't work out just the way you initially planned. But if it's something you love, don't give up on it." Words of wisdom from Bubba.

Few of us will ever have the opportunity to bend history itself. Bubba Bussey is one of those individuals who chased a dream, followed it with all his might, and made things better for himself, his family, and countless other people.

"A tough challenge is just a checkpoint to see if you really want to succeed or you just say that you do." —John Wooden

NEVER GIVE IN

Earlier in the chapter on preparation, we heard from my friend Dr. David Dyson. When I asked David what made the difference for him in overcoming roadblock after roadblock to earn his doctoral degree, he answered, "I learned that writing goals and making promises to prove something to yourself and others helps one persist through adversity and rejection. I firmly believe plans and persistence are more powerful than personality."

David went on to tell me how challenges, burdens, and liabilities can become blessings in two key ways that we often overlook. First, the challenges of life may force us to seek a better path or create a new calling. But our ability to do this is dependent on paying attention to the possibilities before us.

Secondly, a burden provides a platform on which we can develop the ability to be persistently positive under pressure. Here is the way David describes it: "When we admit to and act on burdens, it can help us develop into a 'diamond' of a person—stronger and more valuable than ever before. Added to that is the fact we possess more capacity to take the punches life can throw at us. So, when you face your next big challenge, look past the burden, the liability, the disadvantage to identify the reality of what you can do. Make your focus one on what is needed, what you can do, and the resolve to take positive action as your very best self." Worthy words from Dr. Dyson.

I can assure you that challenges are the one thing we can expect on the road to success. There is nothing worthwhile we do in life in which a significant measure of progress can be made without encountering and conquering significant hurdles along the way. And the farther we travel, the tougher and tougher challenges we can expect to meet. How could you see how much you are worth to yourself if you had no opposition in your way?

Life-Enhancement Message

A real factor in success is the ability to hang on where others tend to let go. A more significant factor is your ability to hang on when you want to let go.

THANKFUL FOR OPPOSITION

"Facing opposition makes things interesting; mastering opposition makes things meaningful."—Stephen Covey

I thoroughly enjoy watching eagles soar. Eagles are a breed unto themselves. From the way they raise their young to the way they prepare for a storm is truly unique. Amazingly, eagles know when a storm is approaching long before it arrives. Prior to the storm's arrival, eagles will fly to some high spot and wait for the winds to come. When the storm hits, eagles set their wings so that the wind will pick them up and lift them above the storm. While the storm rages below, eagles are soaring above. Eagles do not attempt to escape the storm, they simply used the force of the winds to lift them above the storm's fury.

Is there a lesson here for us? When storms come into our lives, have we made plans to rise above them? The storms do not have to overcome us if we are prepared for them. Every one of us has been given the inner strength to lift above the storms we may face in life. We can ride the winds of the storms to new heights. We can soar above them.

One of my favorite Bible verses comes from Isaiah 40:31: "Those who hope in the Lord will renew their strength. They will soar on wings like eagles."

Great challenges and opposition allow our inner qualities to shine, which we may have never known existed otherwise. These challenges simply give us a chance to see what we are made of. They give us a chance to stand up and be counted when the counting counts.

Through the years, I have had the opportunity to rub shoulders with many great achievers. The one constant I discovered about these champions is they reached lofty positions by overcoming tough resistance, be it tangible or intangible. Even when their dreams seemed far from reach, they stayed the course until their intentions were met. These achievers came to grips with the realization that they had what it took to be at their best when the opposition was the stiffest. They learned along the way appreciation for opportunities hidden in difficult challenges. We draw tremendous resources from the difficult opposition we meet. It produces the soil in which we do our best growing and provides us with opportunities for our true potential to shine.

In all walks of life, it is easy to stay the course when conditions are favorable and things are relatively easy to do. But the true test comes when things get a little arduous. You are probably familiar with the old adage "When the going gets tough, the tough get going." But a better approach is this one: When the going gets tough, the tough are already going.

Life-Enhancement Message

When you are facing tough opposition and want to give in, be reminded that winners don't quit and quitters don't win.

—Author Unknown

REMINDERS OF LIFE'S CHALLENGES

- The size of a challenge is no greater than the attitude you have toward overcoming it.

- How high you climb on the success ladder is determined by the rungs of challenges that you overcome.

- The better the results you accomplish, the more challenges you must overcome.

- A tough challenge may delay you temporarily, but only you can stop yourself permanently.

- If you become afraid that you cannot measure up to a challenge, at some point you will live up to that expectation.

- Challenges along the road to success are just guideposts, not stop signs.

- If you look at a challenge as a problem, you will have a problem. If you look at a challenge as an opportunity, you will have an opportunity.

- It may be hard to live with the tough challenges that you encounter, but it's harder to live without them. They give you a chance to see just how good you can be.

- A greater challenge provides you a clearer picture of what you must improve on to enjoy greater fulfillment.

- Don't ever forget: a competitive or challenging situation is a natural habitat for a champion.

The Real Thrill

Is there any real thrill in easy going,
Where your mettle is not proven true?
Where is the joy in achieving that
Which others around you can do?
Now, the greatest satisfaction comes,
And is much sweeter by far to take,
When you overcome a challenge
That you thought you couldn't make.

—Author Unknown

MOVE ON

There is little question that staying power is a much-in-demand virtue. We fuel our staying power for one reason: to finish, to come to a satisfactory conclusion. I reminded salespeople for years that the purpose of what you do is to get to "Yes." The proof will be in the results.

The ability to move on in the face of adverse circumstances is often the key to successful results. It takes tenacity and a deep belief in ourselves to move on toward what we are aiming for.

Yet what happens if we fail to finish and obtain the results we want? There are indeed times in our lives when we should pack our bags and head to the exit. At times it is wise to concede and move on. Often, the secret is in discerning which situations are important and valuable enough to continue versus those that may not be.

Is this specific goal worth pursuing, or should we invest our efforts in something different? Just because we feel strongly about something doesn't mean that it is actually in our best interest. There are times when we think we are being strong and persistent when in fact we are only being stubborn.

There have been times in my life when I have tried to put a round peg into a square hole. I thought it was so important that I succeed at it that I would continually seek a way to make it happen. But to no avail. It is one thing to possess that single-minded, let-nothing-get-in-my-way mentality where we persist with devotion. It is another thing to be bull-headed and allow nothing to deter us from desperately seeking something that is not worthy of our endless pursuit.

Staying the course sometimes means moving on to a different course. It is important to live with the mind-set of being strongly aware that a new path may bring a more just and rewarding conclusion. Use discernment, and learn how to disconnect and undergo introspective evaluation of your ambitions. Disengage from what is going on around you to focus on what is going on within you. Be sensitive to modifying your game plan if a change is ultimately needed in order to fulfill your mission.

SEVENTEEN

FAIL FORWARD

When we fail forward, we have the opportunity
to begin again more intelligently.

Failure is often a misused and ill-defined word, in my mind. Certainly, we all will fail at times, but failing doesn't make us a failure. Failure basically has no objective meaning except that which each of us personally attach to it. A guarantee in life is that we will not succeed in overcoming every challenge. We all realize that the road to success is paved with misfortune and setbacks.

There is little question that I have had my share of setbacks and failures. Let me tell you about one of my biggest failures. The year was 2000. My wife and I bought an antebellum home, circa 1885, with the plans of turning it into a wedding facility and bed-and-breakfast. We visualized it as a monument to greater possibilities. Several months and many thousands of dollars of remodeling later, the doors were opened with pomp and circumstance. On the surface, we had all the makings for success: a beautiful mansion in a small, antique-filled town nestled in the foothills of the Appalachian Mountains. It was a gorgeous setting.

The business was something different than anything I had ever done, something fun. And in the beginning it was. But it did not take long for it to turn out to be anything but fun. We were able to make some progress during the first year. We kept our heads above water. But quickly, beneath all the glitz and glamour, a different story started to unfold.

The ugly undercurrent that was eroding the foundation right out from under us was one familiar to many entrepreneurs. Businesswise, we were simply in over our heads. No doubt, the collateral lack of our understanding of the business started to take its toll. The reality that we did not have the background and experience to make it work slapped us squarely in the face. Enthusiasm and naïveté seldom remain partners for long.

The limits of our knowledge about the business left us to the whim of forces that we had no control over. What decided our fate were the hundreds of small things we knew little or nothing about, things that were vitally important for us to succeed. Our limited knowledge was followed by the aftermath of 9/11 in 2001. Travel dried up, and suddenly people were not getting married at our facility. We discovered that our mousetrap was only trapping us. Our business seemed hopelessly unsalvageable. This underscores the fact that for things to work, any entrepreneur needs more than money and a desire for success.

This is the myth of attraction. The business looks good, but is it the right fit for you? That's the question that's got to be answered. With a $732,000 debt loss and a failed marriage, I got my answer.

If we have done everything in our power to succeed but we ultimately don't, what next? My suggestion would be to let it hurt for a while, but not forever. Feel the sting, learn the lesson, and then move on. We often have a tendency toward suspending the search for a new challenge and the next opportunity because we have labeled ourselves as a failure, but this doesn't have to be the case.

Fortunately for me, I found my next opportunity in the radio business. For fourteen years, I thoroughly enjoyed hosting a daily radio show. I did not recover my financial loss, but I got much more over those years than money could ever give me.

I have discovered that the one thing that sets champions apart is that they use setbacks to do their best growing. Even if they give their best effort and come up short, they have the confidence and determination to right the ship and find new waters.

The lessons taught by the lack of success are the driving force that helps champions redefine and strengthen their future. The glue that holds it all together is mental toughness. It is needed to get us through the rough spots.

RECOVERY CAPACITY

What we do after a big setback is directly determined by our mental attitude, because what we think when we fail will largely determine what we eventually do about it. Our thought process will be the deciding factor in how long it will be until we get back in the saddle and start riding toward future achievements.

We learn how to succeed by first learning how to fail. But where does this learning process begin? It begins with accepting responsibility for our own decisions and actions, by recognizing the reasons why we may be coming up short. We can cite all the reasons why something or someone is causing us to backslide, but it's a bit harder when we face up to our own contributions. Always remember that when you are pointing an accusatory finger at something or someone, there are three pointing back toward you.

Isn't it much easier to lay fault at the feet of something or someone other than ourselves? Playing the victim alleviates our need to self-reflect and own up to dismal results. We also lose the opportunity to learn how to overcome the same hurdles in the future.

We must learn to be accountable for our shortcomings in order to open the door for any form of improvement. We certainly cannot improve on something that we won't admit exists in the first place, can we?

Regardless of the situation, progress always starts with accepting responsibility for what happens in our lives. When we trip and fall, we have to look ourselves in the eye and face up to why we have fallen down. The questions we should be asking ourselves are, *What am I doing about the one thing I can do something about? What am I doing about me?*

In a significant way, progress is a function of using our recovery capacity to bounce back after disappointment strikes. The best way to guarantee failure is not to make the effort to overcome setbacks. Look at it this way: when we are continually facing roadblocks, it is a reflection that we are making every effort to move ahead.

Life-Enhancement Message

The ability to succeed is only as great as the capacity to handle failure. Even the best fail, but what makes them different is what happens after a failure. When they come up short, they don't dwell on it, they learn from it and then move on to the next task.

LEARNING MOMENT

Okay. So you got knocked off your feet? Maybe even knocked down a notch or two? It got the best of you, did it? Now the big question is, what next? What are you going to do about it?

What can I learn from this failure that will help me get back on the right path? is the kind of question we need to find an answer to if we are to make any appreciable progress.

What happens between now and the next major hurdle is crucial to what happens going forward. If we make it a learning moment, then we can take that lesson with us on our next journey. A word of caution: Be careful of letting a stubborn and self-centered attitude get in the way of listening and learning. To either fail to listen or not to buy into the help that is given minimizes the opportunity as a learning moment.

A case in point is Tim Williams. Tim was an outstanding high school running back in football. He had numerous scholarship offers. He settled on one and was set for a great college career. In high school, Tim had developed a habit that was a dead giveaway to the direction he was to carry the ball. If Tim went to his left, he would drop his right foot slightly behind his left. If he was going to his right, his left foot would be slightly behind his right.

This telltale tendency went unnoticed in high school. But at the college level, it was a dead giveaway that allowed the opposing defense to correctly predict the direction of a running play. Coaches did their best to help Tim adjust his foot placement, but to no avail. Tim would politely listen, but he firmly let the coaches know that he had been very successful doing it his way in the past, and continued to do so. As a result, Tim enjoyed little success. Eventually, because he was no longer a significant player on the team, he decided to give up football.

The message is plain as can be: pride can squander opportunities to learn and grow. Those that are too stubborn to seek the help or assistance succumb to that age-old adage "There are none so blind as those who will not listen." The biggest challenge we face when we try to go at it alone is in filling the gap between the availability of quality instruction and the "I'll show 'em" attitude. Many learning opportunities are lost because of this attitude. We could dramatically change the circumstances in our lives simply by seeking out and accepting ways to bring about improved performance.

We haven't utilized all the resources available to us until we maximize every resource that avails itself for a teaching moment. Take advantage of those people who can assist you in taking the next step to bigger and better things. There are people all around you who can be invaluable to your growth. Listen and learn from them. Then perform and reap the rewards.

Life-Enhancement Message

Successful people do not shy away from failure, nor do they never fail. Rather, they are the ones who move forward, who go on despite setbacks, bringing with them the lessons they learned that will minimize the chances of failing again.

YOUR "FORGETTERY"

The one trait that I observed over and over in professional baseball was that those players who had the ability to put the previous play behind them and keep their focus on the present had the most success. This was true whether they had executed a play successfully or just royally messed it up.

This is not to say that those involved didn't demonstrate excitement or disappointment, depending on the results, but that they showed an immediate favorable or unfavorable reaction and then employed their very best "forgettery" and moved on.

Winning the mental struggle in any situation, no matter what the outcome, is the ability to employ our "forgettery." It takes a really conscious effort to wipe the previous situation out of your mind and attach yourself to the next task or situation. A real benefit of having good "forgettery" is that we conserve mental energy. Reacting emotionally, whether to a good or a bad situation, eventually takes a toll on our mental approach. We become increasingly prone to mistakes, and the lack of productivity will be reflected in our current actions. This, in effect, will change the future outcome of whatever we are aiming to accomplish.

Utilizing our "forgettery" helps keep us on an even keel, neutralizing the tendency of emotional swings. We refrain from getting too high or too low. I am not suggesting that we never demonstrate an emotional response. Certainly, there are specific times and places where a reaction is not only appropriate but necessary. We should do it judiciously, though, with emotional stability and purpose. Our "forgettery" will help us do just that.

There is little question that we are not going to reach the pinnacle of every task we undertake. So, when we do come up short, it is vital that we let it become a teachable moment. We learn something from it and then employ our "forgettery" and move on to the next task with increased vigor and mental acumen.

A good "forgettery" is often the difference that helps put us over the top going forward. Those with the best "forgettery" enjoy a greater degree of success than those who fail to stay in the now moment.

Life-Enhancement Message

The most significant feeling you should experience when encountering failure is the inherent awareness of how much you dislike it.

HOW TO FAIL FORWARD

Okay. We know meeting failure on the road to success is inevitable. If there is a truism in this book it is that, to experience success, we have to learn how to handle setbacks. The key here is to make every effort to "fail forward." This emphasizes that we make an attempt to forget about what has happened, learn from it, and focus on what is ahead.

It serves us well to look at failure in a way that will allow us to make every effort to be smarter and stronger than before. To use it as a platform for better execution or decisions in the future is a worthy goal. I hope you can now agree that learning from failure is one of the greatest opportunities we will encounter on our road to success. This learning process involves three very distinct stages:

1. **Awareness stage.** *I should not be doing [whatever needs to be done differently].*

2. **Acceptance stage.** *I should be doing [options of what you should be doing].*

3. **Action stage.** *I will [specify what you will do to bring improvement to your performance].*

Use this formula and you should make great strides in your ability to FAIL FORWARD. Just remember the secret to success is what you do after you have failed.

> ## Life-Enhancement Message
>
> In a competitive situation, always perform on a high enough
> level so that even if you fail to come out on top, you will know
> that someone else succeeded more than you failed.

BE A "SUCCESSFUL FAILURE"

Failure is a breeding ground where we learn what it takes to be successful. No secret there. Since we are well aware that overcoming failure is part of the process of attaining success, it is important that we strive to be a "successful failure." The thought process for a successful failure goes something like this: *When I fail, it doesn't make me a failure. It is just a learning experience and nothing more.*

Willis Magee was a tremendous track star in high school. Charley Hanson, the head football coach, asked Willis if he would come out for the football team to return kickoffs and punts. Willis knew little about football, but he was really fast. That's the reason Coach Hanson wanted Willis on the football team.

"Just catch the ball, son, and run as fast as you can forward." That was Coach's instruction to Willis. So, in his first game, Willis watched the first punt sail over his head. He circled back and picked up the ball inside the ten-yard line. Just as Willis secured the ball he was tackled and he fumbled. The opposing team pounced on the ball at the three-yard line. Two plays later the opponent scored, tying the game at 7–7. While the opposition was scoring, Coach Hanson grabbed Willis on the sideline and told him, "Son, don't ever touch the ball inside the ten-yard line. Give it a chance to go into the end zone for a touchback."

The game was tied 14–14 in the fourth quarter. Another punt was kicked for Willis to return. This one hit Willis on the shoulder pad around the twenty-yard line and rolled toward the end zone. Willis turned and ran wide open to retrieve the fumbled ball until he got to the ten-yard line. You guessed it. He abruptly stopped and watched as the opponents recovered the ball at the two-yard line. The opposing team scored on the first play to go up 20–14, but they missed the extra point.

On the sideline, Coach Hanson was again giving Willis an earful: "What in the world were you thinking? The ball was alive, son! You gotta go get it!"

To which Willis replied, "You told me, Coach, not to pick it up inside the ten-yard line, and I didn't want to make the same mistake twice."

To Willis's credit, he ran the kickoff back for a touchdown, and with a successful extra point, his team won 21–20.

Willis went on to become a star football player in college. He learned something about how to be a successful failure.

Here are some "successful failure" fundamentals:

- Failure is simply a mental ideation, a state of mind.

- Don't ever talk like a failure, for your chances to fail are almost certain then.

- You will be remembered by the times you succeed, not by the times you floundered.

- The more comfortable you get with failure, the easier failure becomes.

- To admit that you were less than your best is a sign of strength, not a confession of weakness.

- Let the past pass. A setback only affects your next task or your next performance when you hold on to it.

All human beings fail on occasion. And since you are a human being, you are going to fail, which means you are only human. Can you be more than that?

EIGHTEEN

LIFE CHANGERS

There are numerous special, intangible gifts that I would gift to you if I could. But that is not necessary because these gifts already are in your possession. They are inbred. You are aware of their presence, but you may not know the extent of their presence. Most likely, you have used all these gifts at varied times under various circumstances. What I would like to gift you is the ability to maximize their use at all times, under all conditions. There is no doubt you have the capability to reach down on the inside and pull them up for regular use. That's where your mental toughness comes into play. When used properly these intangibles help make success a very tangible thing. You got them, just make sure you use them.

My gifts are enthusiasm, energy, excitement, "be where you are," "major in minors," "a little bit more," commitment, courage, heart, and faith. No particular order. They are all worthy of a place in our lives.

ENTHUSIASM

"Enthusiasm defies the laws of mathematics, for when you divide enthusiasm it multiplies."—Cavett Roberts

The origin of the word *enthusiasm* comes from the all-powerful Greek god, Zeus. One who was considered *enthuse* was noted to be with the gods. Enthusiasm has proven to be the stimulus to meaningful action. It is one of those dynamic characteristics that obviously not only affect how we perform, but affect how those around us perform, as well.

When we are enthusiastic, we don't have to wear a sign telling others how we feel on the inside. They see it in our actions. They hear it in our voices. They sense it in our body language. Others can truly recognize the incredible amount of enthusiasm that flows from our lives. They can be drawn to the passion and enthusiasm we evidence on a consistent basis. No question about it: others will even desire to share the enthusiasm we possess. They will want some of the glow and warmth that we bring to our daily activities.

But it is important to note that enthusiasm is one of those traits that cannot be forced. It must be the real deal. It is virtually impossible to be enthusiastic by imitation. That's because enthusiasm is a virtue that arises within our very nature and spirit. It is born of sincere belief in and love of who we are and what we do. Enthusiasm is nurtured by the depths of our knowledge and the precision of our skills. It has grown full boom when it leads us to attack challenges with conviction and determination.

Never underestimate the degree to which enthusiasm plays in obtaining results. Also remember that, while enthusiasm is an individual thing, it is never purely a personal matter. It not only affects your behavior but also plays an important role in the behavior of others.

Without Enthusiasm

All that we say is ineffective.
All that we know is incomplete.
All that we think is insufficient.
All that we believe is insignificant.
All that we do is inadequate.

—Source unknown

ENERGY

When is your high-energy time? Morning, afternoon, or evening? I am a great believer in biorhythms. There are certain times of the day and certain days in the month when my creative juices are more functional. It is important that we arrange our schedule so that we tackle the toughest tasks in our high-energy periods. This may not be possible or even practical for everyone. But when you can, schedule your most demanding tasks when you are most energized and motivated.

One of the first rules in the dictionary of success is to be energized. What can you do to develop and sustain more energy? Here are some suggestions:

- **Think energy.** The first lesson in releasing energy is to "think energy." Within us is enough energy to do what we need to do and what we want to do. All we have to do is access it. This begins with thinking energy, especially when we feel less than energetic.

- **Align with purpose.** The more we are aligned with our purpose for what we do, the less resistance we experience. When we are specific in where we are headed and what we want to accomplish, then we have more energy available to get it done.

- **Stay active.** Energetic people don't waste their time on unproductive thought and activity. They don't sit around using up energy worrying about a coming event. They stay active. Sooner or later, we learn that "the more we do, the more we have to do with."

- **Simulate energy.** We can simulate energy through our body movements and posture. When we walk at a brisk, purposeful pace, look alive and alert, and appear dynamic in all of our activities, we generate energy. The key is for us to keep reminding ourselves that we are a bundle of energy and really mean it.

EXCITEMENT

The mid-1980s saw the emergence of college women's basketball in America. One of the best teams during that period, and for years to come, was the University of Tennessee Lady Volunteers (Vols) coached by the late Pat Head Summit.

I made a presentation to the women's athletic department of the University of Tennessee on the same day the Lady Vols had a home game against Louisiana Tech. Tech was another top women's basketball programs at the time. Both were highly ranked going into the game.

Coach Summit invited me to be a guest "coach" for the game. I sat right behind her on the Lady Vols bench.

At halftime, the Lady Vols were down in the score by seven or eight points. Coach Summit had several choice words for her team in the locker room, but there was one term she kept using that stuck with me: "We have to play with more controlled excitement," Coach Summit emphasized to her team.

What I heard Coach Summit saying was that excessive excitement can be detrimental to performance. Unbridled excitement gets us in over our heads. It leads us to be driven and led by our emotions at the expense of reason and judgment.

Excitement is absolutely necessary. It is a crucial ingredient in any recipe for success. To be genuine, it must arise from the depths of our being. Unless we can feel that tingling on our skin and feel the hair on the back of our necks standing up, we very well may be in the wrong place, doing the wrong thing.

On the other side of the coin, when we are so fired up about the challenge before us that we lose the ability to think clearly and make good decisions, then our excitement will do us more harm than good. Excitement certainly can enhance the level of performance in any task, but it must be kept under control. With controlled excitement, we find ourselves on fire for doing our best, regardless of the situation or the circumstances.

What Coach Summit was talking about is learning how to channel our excitement into ways that will allow us to succeed. It is imperative that we allow common sense to carry us away from a sea of excitement and then learn how to control it.

BE WHERE YOU ARE

"Wherever you are, be there!" Sounds reasonable and achievable, doesn't it?

Why is getting focused and staying focused so crucial to success?

There is a simple answer: because what we focus on, that's where our hearts will be.

Why is the ability to focus and concentrate so difficult to do? The world is full of distractions, making it one of the hardest things to consistently do. Yet we will succeed only in proportion to how diligent we are in "being where we are."

Always remember that the quickest way to get many things done is to do only one thing at once. The vital truth is, unless we direct all energy to one point, we will never perform any task or duty quite as capably as we possibly could. Learning to focus, to concentrate, is an acquired trait. It is impossible to force ourselves to concentrate on anything!

The ability to be focused is derived from the habit of being overly interested in a specific task or challenge. Focus just naturally happens when the interest level is high. Our effectiveness is often dependent in a great part on our ability to block out the distracting things happening around us and within us. When our faculties are not scattered, we are more apt to really get into the swing of things.

The better you focus on the action, the more power and force you will have for achieving quality results. When your concentration is strong, you refrain from remotely considering the possibility that you may not succeed.

MAJOR IN MINORS

There is very little difference between being good and being great in any endeavor. Being great is not necessarily made up of doing the big things, even though they are important. The real difference in attaining greatness is measured by how enthusiastically we stretch to perform the little things that other, less successful people would not think to be worth doing.

Think about it: being a champion is nothing more than a lot of little things done well. In a very real way, it is necessary to major in minors before you can make a dramatic impact in any field. Once we learn how to do the little things well, then we can do the big things that will make us big.

In my years as a professional baseball player, if I learned anything about baseball hitters, it was that there is little difference between top hitters and average hitters.

To illustrate this point, let's say each player participates in 150 games a season and averages four official times at bat (no walks, etc.) each game. That's six hundred times at bat over the course of a baseball season. During the season, the .300 hitter racks up 180 hits and the .250 hitter bangs out 150. That's a difference of thirty hits in 150 games.

Now, if my math is correct, that's one hit every five games, or one hit every twenty times at bat! Doesn't sound like much, does it? But you should see the difference in income. About two and a half times more!

Quite often the little difference that makes a big difference between the two batting averages is their attitude toward the little things. Substantial improvement for the baseball hitter parallels his progress in doing a lot of little things well—learning the strike zone, gaining knowledge of pitchers, hustling on every play, etc.—things that the average player fails to do consistently. Or in many cases, fails to believe he has the capability of doing.

The same holds true in any occupation. Being attentive to the little things that make a big difference in success is a state of mind. It is a kind of ingrained attitude that being great is nothing more than doing a lot of little things well. It is having the belief that big results, more often than not, come through a sustained, persistent effort in the areas that lesser performers overlook or take for granted.

I leave you with these thoughts:

- Attention to little things is no little thing.

- You can only be as big as the little things you let throw you.

- To rise to the top, you have to take care of things at the bottom.

- Don't ever be too big to do the little things that will make you big.

A LITTLE BIT MORE

"Four short words sum up what lifts most successful people above the crowd: a little bit more. They do all that is expected of them, then they do a little bit more."

The "a little bit more" concept was in a book I wrote for young athletes back in the 1990s (*How to Be a Winner: The Young Athletes' Handbook*, Upword Press, 1995). Since then it has been included on several top Internet quote lists.

Another place the "a little bit more" quote could be found in the past few years has been on the desks in the University of Alabama athletic department. Certainly, it helped to contribute to the overall success of the football teams over the years.

Do you really want to step out of the crowd and be something special? Develop the habit of doing something extra by subscribing to the mentality of doing a little bit more. Do you do all that is expected of you and then a little bit more? If you see something that needs to be done, do you wait to be told before doing it, or do you take the initiative and get on with doing it, even if there may be no personal gain in it for you?

Successful people think about how to do things better; not a great deal better, just a little bit better. They turn their attention not only to what needs to be done but instinctively to what is yet to be done. They don't sit back and wait for something to come along to do; they go out and make something happen. They are always working to improve, every day.

An "a little bit more" attitude pays off for everyone. It helps everyone around you feel better about you. It enhances your standing with your colleagues, with your bosses, and with yourself.

An "a little bit more" attitude can give you a big edge in what you do. If you want to get ahead, start taking advantage of those in charge by doing more than they asked you to do, and keep on doing it!

Life-Enhancement Message

*Nothing average ever stood as a monument to progress,
for when progress is looking for a partner, it does not
turn to those who only do what they have to do, it turns to
those who are always striving to do a little bit more.*

COMMITMENT

Your skills and abilities won't get you up in the morning, but your commitment to do your best with what lies ahead will.

How committed are you to what you have chosen to do? Commitment is the common denominator among those who are highly successful in any endeavor. Being successful requires a heart-and-soul effort, and you can only put your heart and soul into something you are committed to. Commitment is active living and a contagious trust in your own ability to achieve the desired goal.

Why do some have a fire in their bellies to give every ounce of talent and boldness to a worthy goal, while others need external stimuli to get their pilot lights lit? Why is it that there are those who never get the internal flame ablaze at all?

It appears that for every person consumed with a commitment to achieve, there's someone else content to accept whatever comes their way. For everyone who is willing to do all that is asked of them and then some, there are those who do just enough to get by.

Which are you? Are you highly motivated to do your very best and then strive to do a little bit more? While there are varied levels and degrees of get-up-and-go, don't let the lack of desire to do well be your downfall.

Commitment is about choices, not conditions. It is about choosing to believe that something can be done. The more committed you are to accomplishing something, the more likely you are to find a way to get it done. A passion for what you are doing is at the heart of commitment. It is this passion that sparks the desire that impels you to do your very best at all times.

Take a closer look at the word *passion*. Break the word down like this: PASS-I-ON. Do you have the kind of passion that is worthy of passing on? When you are inspired by your passion of commitment, your priorities stand out. Your energy and attention are in accord. Your vision has better focus. You use time more effectively and wisely.

Commitment makes tough situations appear less difficult and more doable. It makes obstacles no more than mere hurdles to overcome, while setbacks are seen as simple stepping stones that lead to continued progress.

Nothing great is ever achieved without commitment. I hope you buy into that with all your being.

COURAGE

Our ultimate success is predicated on having the courage to act and get things done. To make an affirmative decision to be courageous is often the difference maker in many of the challenging endeavors we encounter. To be truly successful, courage needs to be our constant companion.

Courage is important on many fronts. It takes courage to rise above the norm, time after time, so we can tap our deepest resources. It takes courage to measure the demands needed to consistently perform well regardless of the challenge we face. When we have the courage to face life's challenges aggressively, they vanish almost as quickly as they appeared.

Do you have the courage to aspire to larger responsibilities? If not, what would it take for the light to come on so you can have the courage to use your talents and abilities to the fullest extent possible?

The reason so many of the things that can change our lives lie dormant is that we haven't exhibited the courage to dig them up and use them. We all have a wealth of possibilities hidden deep in our being, but they will remain unharvested until we display the courage to venture beyond our comfort zone. When we are courageous enough to utilize these great resources, we move toward the greater reward of what can be. We undertake the task to move beyond anything we might have thought we could be.

A word of caution: Courage does not always have carryover value. Courage for one challenge doesn't necessarily mean that it will be automatic for a different type of challenge. We must constantly find the courage to face up to varied challenges as they arise. Things never work out the way we want if we automatically believe that we will be courageous despite the challenge we face.

Set no limits on your ability to act with courage. This attitude alone will help you move toward obtaining the results you want. In a very real way, living courageously and empathically changes the whole complexion of life. Living this way has a lasting kick to it.

When you master the courage equation, you create the right kind of environment to experience growth, happiness, and an appreciation for your capabilities going forward. You make that "someday" you have been waiting for begin to happen today.

Life-Enhancement Message

Momentum is where everything begins to click, and once the surge starts, it is hard to stop. There is no law anywhere that says that a good thing once started cannot be kept going until an adjustment has been made and a goal is achieved. The old saying "All good things must come to an end" is not a truism unless one quits doing all of the "good things" that created the momentum in the first place.

HEART

It is no secret that becoming the very best at any endeavor depends in part on our environment. But the influential limit in maximizing our abilities is something that begins deep within each of our hearts.

Time and time again, results have shown there is apparently something that is not always equal in human beings. Success in any competitive endeavor is not always won by pitting strategy against strategy, strength against strength, skill against skill.

More times than not, competitive events are decided by an intangible factor called heart. The "why" in our hearts will always carry us farther than the "how" in our heads.

Hall of Fame football coach Paul (Bear) Bryant, of the University of Alabama, once said, "Winning is much more about attitude and heart than it is about talent and ability."

I would venture that in any endeavor, our heart muscle is our strongest muscle. No doubt, talent is what we possess, but heart is what possesses us.

When everything else is about equal, the biggest difference between success and failure at anything we do will be about a foot, which is roughly the difference from our heads to our hearts.

Nothing is cut in stone about how to insert more heart into our efforts. It truly is a personal thing. It is such an intangible that it strikes right at the core of much of what we talk about in this book.

Some would say that you either have it or you don't, but I believe heart power can grow over time. It is a product of our purpose, goals, values, and beliefs. The lifeblood of heart is to get excited and to stay excited.

Life-Enhancement Message

Others can measure how tall you are and how much you weigh; they can measure the strength in your body and the level of your skills; they can measure the depth of your knowledge and the apex of your intelligence, but they cannot measure the size of your heart. Only you can measure that!

FAITH

Someone very aptly described faith as an acronym: forsaking all I trust him. Those of us who believe in the power of faith through prayer seek God's guidance and direction in dealing with the challenges of health issues and many undefined fears and phobias.

Some would tell me that the results of prayer are not provable. I like to think that the deepest truths of life never are. The best things of our existence are believed, not known. That is the backbone of faith.

Faith is difficult to define accurately. But I am aware that managing fear through faith not only demonstrates our faith, it develops our faith, as well.

A friend and I were hitting tennis balls when a young lady jogged by on the walking/running track located by the tennis court. Nothing unusual about that, except this young lady was virtually bald. "There must be a real story here," I murmured under my breath. My radio-talk-show instincts were taking over.

So, the next time she headed by the courts, I interrupted her jogging and asked if we could talk. She told me as she raced by that we could talk after she finished her run. True to her word, Bethany Albritton returned for a conversation. Bethany confirmed what I suspected. Only six weeks before, she had been treated for cancer. She didn't tell me then about her bout with the horrible disease; she later did in an interview on my radio show. Here is Bethany's story in her own words:

> Bethany Faith Albritton is my full name. I believe even at birth faith was given to me because only God knew that I was going to walk through some dead, dry places in my life.
>
> The summer of 2016 began with the loss of an earring that was very personal, and very valuable, to me. But God spoke to my inner spirit these words: "When you lose those things you deem as valuable, I'll replace them with things you'll never lose."
>
> I wrote these words down on the back of an old envelope for safekeeping. I did not understand what it meant at the time, but it would soon become an anchor for me through a mighty storm.
>
> The storm for me arose in August 2016. It was called ovarian cancer. It blew up into my life like one of those unexpected summer storms.

A twelve-pound mass the size of a cantaloupe was attached to an ovary. It caused all my female organs to be rearranged. Everything had to be removed during surgery.

I would say we all would fear to take on the "cancer" title. I started to understand the fear of fighting cancer more and more, firsthand.

The words of my mom ring true. She said at the beginning of the cancer battle, "Bethany, good sailors don't come from smooth waters." We all want to be good, but we want to skip the storm, don't we?

I have a whole new insight into this battle . . . sometimes daily fighting the thoughts it brings. I fight those fears with my faith in my Lord and Savior, Jesus Christ.

Even when I talk with another cancer survivor and fear tries to sneak in, I stand on His promises. I firmly believe Jesus has a step-by-step plan for me.

One of my biggest fears was losing my hair after taking the chemo treatments. I lost it. It fell out in handfuls every time I brushed it.

Losing my hair was devastating at first, but from it came a great lesson for my daughters, Lylia and Temple. I never want them to look in the mirror and ever feel that their beauty comes from their hair. Beauty is much deeper than that.

I want to share a quote from an unknown source I recently heard that paints a true picture concerning the last few years of my life: "My darkest days have become my greatest days."

The journey I shared with you I am grateful for. I would have hated to have lived the rest of my life without the "gold nuggets" that God gave me in the dark places of my journey!

It was through the bad times, all the pain and the fear, the loss, the tears, the trust, the comfort, the strength, that I believe these ""gold nuggets" arose. You see, we don't learn from our perfection but from our scarred lives.

I still have checkups every three months. As I write this, another one of my three-month checkups is upon me. I tend to get emotional a week before we go, but this time I feel different. My faith is deeper and stronger than ever.

Bethany had to call on remarkable courage, strong faith, and a loving and caring family. Her devoted husband, Tim, and her four beautiful children, Lylia, Temple, Silas, and Shepard, have been pillars of strength for Bethany.

All cancer survivors live with the horrible truth that cancer may return. They have to deal with the uncertainty, the doubt, the anxiety, the insecurity, and the fear that lie in the aftermath. But Bethany's faith in the future is inspiring to all who know her. I have a feeling it will inspire many others in the future, as well. This brave, dedicated lady has demonstrated that through faith one can stand up to anything.

NINETEEN

RIGHT IS RIGHT

If life is tough for us, it could well be that we are false with life.
The art of living requires honesty, integrity, and realism.
—George Christian Anderson

Our character and reputation will make us or break us. Character is what we are, our private substance. Reputation is what others think we are, our public image. A reputation is a message about us that grows and travels by word of mouth. Yet reputation is a fragile thing. It can be easily fractured should we compromise on character. Upright character is the only sound foundation for a solid reputation.

The events of daily life not only build character, they reveal character. If we do not possess the major ingredient of character—integrity—it is easy to compromise on honesty and truthfulness.

Integrity is an unrelenting demand to do our best within the confines of the rules and regulations. It cannot be achieved by doing the right thing in short bursts to satisfy the whim of the moment. It is doing what is ethically right all the time.

Unbridled ambition can lead to highly unethical practices. There has to be an effective compromise with success at a high cost, but not at any cost. The secret is to strive for balance. One of the most demanding forms of mental toughness is to make decisions we can live with tomorrow, not on what we might get away with today. Life calls for constant vigilance. It depends on a mind-set that is attuned to integrity.

We are the sum total of our actions, to the very end. Integrity cannot be counterfeited. It cannot be put on or taken off, like a garment, to meet the whim of the moment. Like the markings that are ingrained in the very heart of a tree, integrity is fostered and made evident by what we are on the inside. The marvel of integrity is that it can be developed and nurtured. It begins with having a clear picture in mind of the kind of person we want to be and then acting according to that image.

Listen carefully to these words from an unknown source:

> Watch your thoughts, for they become words.
> Watch your words, for they become actions.
> Watch your actions, for they become habits.
> Watch your habits, for they define character.
> Watch your character, for it establishes your destiny.

VALUES REVISITED

Every day, we meet life situations that challenge us to decide what is right or wrong, good or bad, just or unjust. Some of these situations are routine. Some are unique. Others are a matter of importance. It is our value system that determines what choices we make in every situation. The dictionary defines *values* in this manner: "Values are preferences we have about what is desirable in life situations." Values are stable, longlasting standards by which we make choices and bring order to our lives.

Our values guide us and shape our priorities and reactions. They serve as indicators to let us know if we are headed in the right direction, if what we are doing is right.

Here are some of the values I believe are important to all of us: accountability, creativity, authenticity, truthfulness, appreciation, dependability, patience, tolerance, concentration, generosity, self-reliance, exploration, and caring. That's a lucky thirteen.

When our actions and words are aligned with our values, life is generally good and we feel content, confident, and satisfied. But when our behaviors don't match up with our values, we soon begin to sense an uneasiness that starts to swell and grow inside of us.

Developing values is a do-it-yourself project. Certainly, what happens around us has a bearing on what happens within us. But the ultimate reason for building a quality value system arises from the best that's within us.

That's the way it should be, but is that truly the way it is today? Many have known (or still know) what it is like to join the crowd and turn to indulgence and diversions that are the popular fads of the day. When we are chasing what is in vogue, the search is for something to satisfy a restlessness and hunger for meaning and direction in life. Some find these things satisfying to varying degrees. But these pleasurable experiences are only momentary, and then it is on to something else, to the next temptation, and the search for life's purpose moves on with it.

Temptation moves us away from what we know to be right. Even in the face of wanting to do the right thing, a blind spot develops. It grabs hold of us and leads us in the wrong direction. Once that happens, it is extremely difficult to find our way back.

VALUES AND TODAY'S YOUTH

From an adult standpoint, our world was not as complicated as the one faced by today's young people. In many ways, we experienced many of the same temptations, but not to the same degree. Our young people function in a world that tugs and pulls at them from all sides. What are they to believe? Who are they to believe?

In a society that makes confusing and conflicting demands, developing an upright and solid value system is often difficult. What are young people to do today to possess a system of values that can help them negotiate the complicated maze called life? What can adults do to help them? Adults must emphasize to young people the importance of asking themselves these types of questions: *What will be the consequence of the next choice I make? Will it increase me or decrease me?*

Is it right or wrong? Young and older people alike need to understand that almost right is wrong.

For every choice any of us make, there is a consequence. If you are a parent or grandparent, make it a habit of raising the question of choices and consequences every time a young person walks out the door. Emphasize to them that if they do this or that, here are the possible consequences.

Values are personal. The choice of what gives meaning and direction to life is dependent on each individual person. But God gave us something to assist each of us in making the right choice. He placed a little thing down deep in the pit of our stomachs. I call it "the gnawer."

When we don't do right, it gnaws, gnaws, and gnaws at us. Whether we are young or old, we should listen to our gnawer. It is our best self-talking to us.

NOTHING BUT THE TRUTH

Do you attempt to be truthful to everyone you meet and converse with on a daily basis? We should stand firm on the level ground of truth with everyone, everywhere.

Here are some reminders about truth with a twist of wit:

- Truth doesn't hurt unless it ought to.

- Be careful of stretching the truth: it might snap back.

- Better suffer for the truth than to be rewarded for a lie.

- The truth may turn out to be expensive, but in the long run, we can afford it.

- Truth never wobbles. If the truth needs crutches, it is not the whole truth.

- With truth in the heart, there is no need for persuasion on the tongue.

- Beware of a half-truth: you don't know which half you are going to get.

- The person who says there is no such thing as an honest person probably just identified one who is not.

The sun shines on the honest and dishonest alike. But I think we can say with certainty that the day of reckoning comes for those who have a problem telling the truth.

As the ancient saying goes, "You can fool some of the people some of the time, but you can't fool all the people all the time."

TRUE TO YOURSELF

The sidewalks are full of people wearing the most up-to-date clothes and the most exquisite jewelry. They shop in the most expensive stores. They are seen in the best restaurants. But what do we see when we examine their lives? Do they hide behind this misleading guise of external trappings? Are they wearing their personalities on their backs? Are they living a lie to themselves?

Being explicit about who we are is to admit to ourselves these words: *I'm human. Like all humans, I have self-doubts, insecurities, and fears. But I understand that although I feel these things, I'm no less of a person.*

When we step up and admit our shortcomings, we put ourselves in a position to do something about them. Any attempt to continue to hide them is to be false with ourselves. Being honest and truthful with ourselves is not easy, but it is important if we are to make the necessary steps toward building a better life.

Nowhere is truth more important than being true to one's self. How do you know when your reality is out of line with what is really true?

Take the case of Demetris "Sarge" Robinson. According to military records, Sarge is a war hero. He won the Bronze Star for heroism and also is a recipient of a Purple Heart for injuries received in the Vietnam War. But Sarge told me, "I'm anything but a hero." Here is his story.

It was November 1969. Sarge and his squad found themselves surrounded by the enemy, and all but one of them were able to find cover in a bunker. Unfortunately, that one soldier was the radio contact person. He fell about twenty yards from the bunker and appeared to be mortally wounded. Without radio contact to call for air support, the whole squad would probably perish. Someone had to do something soon to retrieve the radio.

Suddenly, Sarge bolted from the bunker to secure the radio in order to make contact. Once the radio was in his hands, he immediately called for reinforcements. Bullets were zinging by him from all directions. Here's Sarge's account of what happened next: "I didn't know whether or not the radio man was dead or alive. I knew without the radio we would not make it. I was just a nineteen-year-old kid who wanted to live.

I had started to turn back toward the bunker without him when he opened his eyes. He couldn't talk, but I knew what he wanted; he wanted me to take him with me. Those eyes would have haunted me for the rest of my life if I hadn't."

Without hesitation, Sarge hoisted the wounded soldier on his back and moved as quickly as he could toward the bunker. The bullets were still ringing out all around them. Sarge was just a few yards from temporary safety when he felt a burning sensation in his side. Blood began to gush out. Now wounded himself and racked with pain, Sarge struggled with all his might to make it to the bunker. Eventually, the two soldiers were behind the shelter, both seriously wounded.

Sarge's radio message had gotten through. Soon there were friendly helicopters all around. The squad was air-lifted to safety, and both the wounded men were off to the hospital.

As Sarge finished telling me his story, he reemphasized, "I was nobody's hero. Everything I did in Vietnam was just so that I would survive. Now, see why I'm no hero. I was worried about my own skin, not anyone else's."

I got the feeling that Sarge's emotions have tossed and turned on the restless sea of time for the past sixty years. The officer who wrote the report citing Sarge's heroism and bravery witnessed the whole event.

Is Sarge being true to himself about this traumatic incident in his life? He does not believe he is a hero because his original intentions were simply to save himself. But the eyes of the wounded soldier brought out the true nature of Sarge, didn't they?

Sarge suffered from post-traumatic stress disorder after returning home from Vietnam. He even attempted to commit suicide, but survived to lead a very productive life. He returned to college, got his master's degree in education, and spent twenty-five years as a coach and teacher.

The correct way to right wrongs in our lives is to admit our human frailties. When we are true to ourselves, improvement of any magnitude is definitely easier to come by. On the other hand, failing to be honest with ourselves makes us a slave to our failings.

This is real in everything we do in life: What we sow is what we reap. Day by day we write our destiny. Are we honest with who we are?

TAKE THE HIGH ROAD

Have you listened to yourself lately? Are you spending valuable time complaining about everything under the sun? Complaining is as old as the human species itself. Now, I would be the first to admit there are some things and conditions we should complain about. But the biggest challenge is when complaining becomes a habit, when we are always griping and whining about this or that.

Have you ever wondered why most complainers complain? The primary reason is because they dislike the direction of their lives. They are coming up short on results, and the individual complainer is not the problem. It is always something or someone else that is holding them back.

We should remember that we can't complain and make positive things happen at the same time. Put differently: we can't rock the boat and row it at the same time. Make sense?

THAT'S NOT FAIR

One of the complaints I hear on a regular basis is this one: "That's just not fair!" Or a different version would sound like this: Life is just not fair! But who says things are supposed to be fair?

Little to nothing in life is designed to be fair. To survive and then thrive, we must learn to deal with situations and conditions that appear to be less than fair. The truth is that a lot of us have our own set of problems and challenges that we view as unfair, and some have more burdens to bear than others.

Unfair or not, whatever hand is dealt to us, we must play it to the best of our abilities. Fairness is when we take what appears to be an unfair situation and turn it into a plus situation. That's the reality of it, and that's the only way to level the playing field.

BYE-BYE, COMPLAINTS

If you have a complaint about people, things, or conditions, offer it with a suggestion of how things can be improved. Don't complain about how bad things are without providing something of substance that can remedy the situation. If complaining is something you need to address personally, then start looking for the good first. There is a tad of good in every situation. Find it.

Most complaints are voiced before we have given something a fair trial. The wise move is to be solution minded, not problem minded. Think in terms of what you can do to correct the situation, long before offering a complaint about it. Do something about the things you can change, and learn how to live with those you cannot change.

It will be amazing how much better you will feel about those situations you find yourself constantly complaining about. Use your time to build things up, not tear them down.

Life-Enhancement Message

You can't row the boat and rock the boat at the same time.

—Dr. Frank Crane

PASSING THE BUCK

When things are not going our way, isn't there a tendency to "pass the buck"? It is relatively easy to blame someone or something else when we come up short. Passing the buck is just another way of testing our integrity. All it does is prolong dealing with reality. Whatever the situation, an alibi will do nothing to change the reality of the situation.

Do you know where the first recorded incident of passing the buck is located? It is found in the Bible in the first chapter of Genesis. The scene finds Adam and Eve in the Garden of Eden. As the plot unfolds, Eve is confronted by a sleek-looking, smooth-talking serpent who talks Eve into eating fruit from a forbidden tree that God had previously told Adam and Eve was off limits to them. Being the good partner, Eve passes the sweet, juicy fruit along to Adam, who also enjoys it.

Shortly, realizing their sin, both try to hide from God. But as they should have known, there is no hiding from Him. God sternly inquires of Adam, "Have you eaten of the fruit from the forbidden tree in the garden?"

Adam immediately reaches for an alibi, "The woman that you gave to me, she gave me the fruit and I did eat." Adam has just uttered the first incident of passing the buck.

Notice here that Adam passed the buck in two directions: First, he implied that God was partly responsible, for it was the woman He gave to him that first created the problem. Adam implied that maybe God should have checked her references a little better. Then He would have known better than to dispense her to be with him in such unprecedented surroundings. But Adam wasn't finished. He implicated Eve, indicating that if she had not provided the fruit, he wouldn't have eaten it.

What about Eve? She didn't bear up any better. She pointed the guilty finger at the serpent. It was the serpent who started the ball rolling in the first place.

Through the ages, we find that the technique of passing the buck hasn't been improved upon very much. An alibi is still an alibi.

Life-Enhancement Message

Nothing inhibits progress more than making excuses and passing the blame. The moment we search for an excuse for poor performance is the moment we limit the possibilities for future success in that area of life. If our first impulse is to make excuses for our shortcomings, we will rarely do anything to change those shortcomings. Please understand, when you find fault with all that you see, it's time to ask yourself, "What's wrong with me?"

—Dr. Marv Levy, Pro Football Coach

APPLAUD OTHERS

I shared my thoughts on comparisons in an earlier chapter. I want to take that theme in a different direction. It is not all bad when beginning something new and different to use the performances of others as a means of measurement. Others in similar situations establish the ground rules and provide a yardstick.

But once we know the rules, we should turn our attention to what we are doing, not what others are doing or have done. When the focus is on the performance of others, we lose sight of what we are capable of doing. I have discovered that champions don't waste time and energy concerning themselves with how others are performing. They don't lie awake at night thinking about things like *Is someone else getting ahead faster, getting more attention from the boss, making more money?*

How can we live up to our own potential when we are always concerned with what others have accomplished or the attention they are getting? We also saw in an earlier chapter that we can rest assured that the envy of others is a direct path to mediocrity.

One of the hardest lessons for any of us to learn is to stand up and applaud the success of others and really mean it. An envious nature is highly detrimental to the ability to perform at a peak level. A useful strategy is to redirect our feelings of envy and concentrate only on bettering our own performance. In that way, we will be focusing on fulfilling our own potential.

Our least concern should be whether we are better or worse than others. No matter how good we are at what we do, there is probably someone who can do it a little better. They may have more talent, more resources, or more experience; but just because they have more doesn't mean we have less, does it?

What others achieve doesn't diminish the opportunities available to us. There's room in this world for all of us to fulfill our potential and become the very best we possibly can be at something. Only one valid comparison really counts: the comparison between who you are and where you are and what we are capable of becoming and where we are capable of landing.

Success doesn't mean getting ahead of others. It means getting ahead of yourself. It means doing things you haven't done before with the expectation of experiencing results you never imagined you could experience.

I would like to leave two thoughts with you about the importance of doing things right because it is right:

- First, do what you have to do and do it well even if there isn't a single soul in sight.

- Secondly, do what you do in such a way that it will bring praise from the person whose opinion counts the most: YOU.

TWENTY

HIGH EMOTIONAL QUOTIENT

Has your temper ever landed you in the spotlight for the wrong reasons? Mine has. My professional baseball career took a turn for the worse because of my inability to keep my cool. Let me explain.

It was an important game for me. Scouts from a major league team were in the stands for the sole purpose of exploring a possible trade. I was to be one of the principals in the trade. I completely lost it over a bad call on a ball-and-strike situation by the umpire. It was at a crucial point in the game. There were two strikes on the batter, and I threw a pitch that appeared to be an obvious strike but was called a ball by the umpire. Both our manager and catcher were thrown out of the game because of their choice comments about the umpire's eyesight.

Nothing unusual about players being upset and arguing over an umpire's call. But you have to get over it and move on.

I didn't. And my lack of focus on the next pitch cost me dearly. It was a game-winning home-run pitch. Then my wrath toward the umpire was even more unpleasant, to say the least. I blew it. I simply didn't stand up to Lou. The result: there was no trade, and no opportunity to go to a major league team at that point in time.

I hope you haven't experienced anything that dramatic, but so many of us have let our temper get the best of us at one time or another.

Do you have a tendency to lose your temper when things don't go your way? Do you fly off the handle when someone does something or says something you don't like? Do you easily become angry with yourself when you are not performing as well as you know you can? Unless you maintain a firm grip on these emotions, they can carry you farther and farther away from the mainstream of life.

EYES OF THE EMOTIONS

Most of us would like to think reason and sound judgment play the dominant role in how we conduct our daily affairs. But in truth, almost everything we do is interpreted at the emotional level. In a very real way, we see and do things through the eyes of our emotions. The word *emotion* comes from the Latin word *exmovere*, meaning "to excite, to stir up, or to move." Emotions are a basic and essential part of life.

Through the years, one of the things I have noticed about the top achievers is their emotional control. While they experience the depth and breadth of a life of emotions, they have a really good handle on them. They have an element of consistency about themselves, which brings balance to their emotional life. This doesn't mean they always refrain from having their negative emotional moments. They experience them, but they don't let them take over; they don't dwell on them. They deal with them and then move on to more constructive feelings.

Neither do the top performers get overly charged. They have a calmness and easiness about themselves that serve to keep their equilibrium as they move through the process of living. They exercise composure in those situations where constraint is vital to high performance.

That's the reason I believe a high emotional quotient (EQ) will move us up the success ladder quicker than will a high IQ. It would be great to have both, but highly developed people display great emotional control and stability.

If we are going to enjoy any significant success, it is essential that we balance reason with emotion. It is precisely the ability to experience the whole range of human emotions at the right time, and in the right degree, that will dramatically impact our efforts in a positive way.

Balance is so important because the body cannot defend itself against the damage that emotional stress creates quietly over time. The body pays a higher physiological price for every additional moment that we feel anxious, tense, frustrated, or angry. While these emotions serve important purposes for us on appropriate occasions, over time they take a heavy toll on the body.

As you probe your own experiences, what can you say about the role emotions are playing in your own career or life? How are you doing in the area of emotional control and stability? Are your emotions working for or against you? Are your emotions your best servant or your worst enemy?

Life-Enhancement Message

Your deeds, not your words, will be your greatest monument to others.

KEEP YOUR COOL

I don't mean to make light of keeping your cool, but here are some humorous ideas from various unknown sources that can help:

- The more you grow up, the less you will blow up.

- Flying into a rage always results in unsafe landings.

- Those who are always exploding rarely end up being big shots.

- It's more tasteful to swallow angry words before we say them than to eat them afterward.

- Those folks who lose their heads are the last ones to find them.

- We are more apt to remain calm and collected when we show restraint in shooting from the lip.

- We contribute to the world's pollution problem when we blow our stacks.

- The trouble with letting off steam is that it only gets us into more hot water.

- Others find out what kind of mind we have when we give them a piece of it.

- Before giving someone a piece of your mind, just make sure you can get by with what's left.

- Striking while the iron is hot is good. Striking while the head is hot is *not*.

"IT'S OKAY" ATTITUDE

It took me years to discover that one of the best ways to maintain emotional control is to key in on an "it's okay" attitude. This attitude is built on the premise that if there is nothing I can do about a situation, then why should I get emotionally involved with it?

Few of us are immune to the little things that can get under our skin and endanger our emotional well-being. The traffic jam on the way to work, the driver in front of us going ten miles below the speed limit, a business associate who is late on a project, a spouse who is upset because a chore has not been done . . . the list goes on.

Isn't it really okay for the world to move at its own pace? If you get upset, what have you achieved? When the driver ahead of you is daydreaming and causes you to miss a green light, and you are already late for an important appointment, what do you do? Do you blow your car horn and blow your stack? What have you truly accomplished with this kind of action? Are you going to let someone else's conscious or unconscious action knock you out of your "it's okay" state of mind?

How about that flat tire? How do you react to it? Just let it be okay, get out the jack and spare and fix it, or call for help? We can get upset and angry and feel miserable, but guess what? The tire still needs to be changed, doesn't it?

The obese person worries about weight. Where is the focus? Isn't it on the weight, not on the solution? When we worry, we visualize the problem, not the solution. By picturing the weight issue continuously in their minds, that's what the obese people get: more weight.

The first law in overcoming any problem is to first view it as being okay. When we allow our problems to be okay, we have positioned ourselves to move beyond the problem and begin the process of seeking an answer or solution. The goal is simple: adjust to the realities of life regardless of how unfair these realities appear to be. An "it's okay" attitude helps us do that.

A roommate of mine in pro baseball often used the term "You gotta cooperate with the inevitable." Learn to go with the flow. Let things be. Cooperate with the inevitable. Establish an "it's okay" attitude. If you do, you will last longer and go farther.

EMOTIONAL INHIBITORS

There are over six hundred words in the English language that express negative feelings. I think I have known some people who have used every one of them in a very short period of time.

Negative emotions are part of life. This is a given. Unpleasant feelings are just as crucial as the enjoyable ones in helping us get a handle on life's ups and downs. If it weren't for a few negative emotions now and then, we wouldn't enjoy the good ones as much, would we?

Think with me a minute. Certain situations, like losing a job, experiencing a tumultuous marriage, facing monetary issues, or witnessing the death of a loved one, lead to some kind of negative reaction. The depth of the reaction we internalize about negative situations can lead to health issues.

It has been my experience that attempting to suppress negative emotions can backfire and even diminish our sense of well-being. Instead of backing away from negative emotions, it is crucial that we accept them and manage them. The way we deal with emotions, especially negative ones, has very important consequences. Emotions come. Emotions go. The aftermath holds the key. Some negative emotions can take us down to unbearable depths.

Nevertheless, there are times when negative emotions can play a role in our survival. Our outlook can become so rosy that we may ignore danger signs, or become complacent to vital clues about important health-and-wellness matters that need attention. Although positive emotions can be a key factor in both attaining and maintaining mental health, research shows that how we go about handling negative emotions also plays a vital role in our well-being. Hopefully, if this is a concern for you, you will gain greater clarity in how to face up to negative emotions.

FROM NEGATIVE TO POSITIVE

How effective are you in taking a highly negative situation and generating a positive from it? This ability to make "the switch" is vital to mental well-being. A lot of the guests I had on my radio show had great stories to tell. None were more impressive than David Rubin's story.

Not many of us will ever face the type of situation that David and his young son, Ruby, encountered as they returned home to Shiloh, Israel, from Jerusalem. They were ambushed by terrorists on December 17, 2001. The attack was sudden and vicious. Gunshots rang out all around the car, and both David and Ruby were struck by bullets from an AK assault rifle.

Ruby was shot in the back of his neck. The bullet missed his brain stem by one millimeter. David was shot in the leg. As he describes it, "Blood was gushing out like an open hydrant." But the two faced an even greater problem: the car went totally dead. David repeatedly turned the ignition, and the car failed to start as a hail of terrorists' bullets continued to fly around them. Miraculously, the car finally started, and David somehow managed to rush himself and his son to a hospital. Both survived, recovered, and today lead normal lives.

Now for the rest of the story. David, who served as mayor of Shiloh, Israel, vowed to fight back against terrorism. He established the Shiloh Israel Children's Home. The home has helped countless youngsters heal from the trauma of terrorism. Innocent children who have lost loved ones or witnessed the horror of terrorism firsthand found a place where they could be children again.

David Rubin's response to the long-term effects caused by Islamic terrorism was one of turning evil into good. The Shiloh Israel Children's Home has been a blessing to hundreds of youngsters. I miss my radio conversations with David, but I occasionally catch him on a national TV show talking about the historical and current facts of the biblical heartland.

The story of David, Ruby, and the Children's Home has served as an inspiration to thousands around the world. The Children's Home is a monument to courage and one man's desire to stand up to those who have shown little regard for humanity.

David's emotional feelings toward the terrorists has not changed. The switch he made was to create something very positive from a very negative situation. The world needs more David Rubins.

GUILT

I want us to take some time to look at a handful of emotions that appear on a rather consistent basis in life: guilt, forgiveness, and grief.

Guilt is an emotion that has at its base anger toward one's self. *You should be ashamed of yourself* or *You really blew it, didn't you?* These are the type of guilty messages that arise in the conscience. The function of the conscience is to differentiate the good from the bad. Guilty feelings develop when all we see is the bad.

Guilt comes in many forms. The most obvious form of guilt arises when we realize we have actually done something wrong, when we have violated our own ethical code of conduct or moral standards. Even contemplating an act that violates our standards can be as guilt provoking as the act itself.

Guilt also arises when we fail to obtain something we wanted or expected to get. Coming up short on results can leave us with a personal guilt hangover. Guilt is made even more real when we didn't do enough to help someone. These guilty feelings are even more pronounced when we are internally convinced that we have caused harm or been responsible for someone else's physical or psychological pain.

Hiram Johnson is a friend. He is a clinical social worker/ therapist who has spent over twenty-five years helping individuals cope with many and varied negative emotions, including guilt. Guilt is something that Hiram had a great amount of personal experience with. His book *Tragic Redemption: Healing the Guilt and Shame* (Langmarc Publishing, 2006) details his personal story about survivor guilt. Hiram was in his junior year in college when he was involved in a tragic automobile crash. He was distracted by a passenger while driving the vehicle, and the resulting accident caused the death of a young lady who was a passenger in his car.

In his book, Hiram details his long trip through depression, shame, guilt, and doubt that led to psychiatric hospitalization. Fortunately, through the grace of God, he emerged on the other side a person with a tremendous desire to use his life experience to aid others. He has done that well. Few will ever have the horrifying experience that Hiram Johnson did, but many of us have felt at times like giving up because of the guilt we experienced as a result of the bad treatment or neglect of another human being.

Guilty feelings can consume us with hopelessness and despair. Negative thoughts can run rampant. It would not be unusual to basically give up at this stage. But I think Hiram would be the first to remind us that giving up will not change the circumstances. As hard as it may be, our own tragic mistake will not help bring someone back to life nor, in most cases, change painful inflictions

His story is one that reflects the transformation from abject survivor guilt to a feeling of helpfulness and wholeness. Presently, Hiram is a professional counselor who has counseled countless people who have suffered from psychological and emotional challenges, many of whom have suffered from situations of their own making.

Hiram Johnson's story might just be the tonic to inspire you to muster the mental fortitude and acumen to do something about your guilt. There are no concrete rules for dealing with guilt. Dealing with the hard feelings that guilt brings is not easy, but it can be done.

The first step is to clarify why there are guilty feelings. The next step is to define what sort of self-assurance is needed to tackle the guilt issue. From this start, we can acknowledge what kind of involvement is needed in turning things around. In many situations, the ability to forgive ourselves lies at the core of moving on beyond guilt. This is often the hardest kind of forgiveness, but it is needed to keep us moving onward and upward. Once we liberate ourselves from the guilt trip we have been on, our world will get brighter and more full of possibilities. Before we know it, life will appear challenging and exciting rather than overwhelming.

FORGIVENESS

There is an old saying that the largest load you can carry is a grudge. You have probably heard this one, too: "Holding a grudge is like taking poison, then waiting around for the other person to die."

Are you hanging on to any old grudges? Grudges are those emotional boomerangs that make it back into our lives, one way or another.

Colonel Glenn Frazier, who passed away in 2018, was a frequent guest on my radio show. A World War II veteran, Colonel Frazier suffered through one of the most notorious of all war crimes, the Bataan Death March. The Bataan Death March was the forcible removal in 1942 by the Japanese Army of between of sixty thousand and eighty thousand American and Filipino prisoners of war. An estimated ten thousand to eighteen thousand of the prisoners perished on the sixty-plus-mile trip. Most of those who fell in the roadway were crushed by Japanese motorized equipment.

Colonel Frazier, then barely seventeen years old (he lied about his age to get into the service), survived the eight-day, seven-night march. He spent the remaining years of the war laboring in a Japanese concentration camp. It was not until after the war ended that anyone was aware Frazier was still alive.

Colonel Frazier returned home to begin life anew, and he brought something with him from Japan. Buried deep in his psyche was a strong and abiding hatred of the Japanese, which he would carry around for years. Colonel Glenn Frazier retired from the military as a sergeant. He was awarded an honorary colonel designation by his native state of Alabama. Regardless of his rank, Colonel Frazier served his country well. He was the recipient of a Bronze Star and four Purple Hearts.

Colonel Frazier joined me on my radio show to talk about his book *Hell's Guest*. He wrote about the transition he made from extreme bitterness to complete forgiveness. The chore of ridding himself of the tremendously bad feelings he had for the Japanese was a long and arduous ordeal for Colonel Frazier. His hatred and bitterness ran deep. But the colonel found in his heart the courage to forgive his captors. He even returned to Japan and met with some of those who had worked in the concentration camp where he was held.

Learning how to forgive is one of the toughest lessons to learn. If we hang around this old earth long enough, we are going to have ample reasons to carry an abundance of grudges. We also will have many opportunities to forgive.

Forgiveness is not something we do for others, it is something we do for ourselves. It is something that involves both attitude and action. Since forgiving some of the hurts we have experienced is not easy, we may need to act the part. What I am saying is, if we find it hard to forgive someone, act forgivingly. Tell the individual you have wronged that you would like to heal the relationship. Then act the part if you must. Send an appropriate email. Offer a helping hand on a project. Schedule a lunch. Send a gift. Many times, we discover that the right attitude will lead to the right actions and end up leading to the right feelings.

I want you to really focus on these words: In whatever area of life that you fail to forgive others, you will block your ability to truly enjoy success and going forward. Give it up. Forgive in order to move on freely.

Life-Enhancement Message

Forgive those who have wronged you—not because it might change their hearts, but because it's more likely to change yours.

GRIEVING

One of the places where emotions play a significant role is in the grieving process. In a time of bereavement, we have the opportunity to be an encouraging force to others.

Elizabeth Chryst is the author of *The Little Blue Book of Grieving*. She lost her husband, Ron Letchworth, at age sixty-two, in 2011. *The Little Blue Book of Grieving* was written to help others navigate the grieving journey.

Elizabeth was a weekly contributor on my radio show for almost nine years. From 1975 to 2001 Elizabeth served as the secretary for the Republican Party in the US Senate. During her twenty-six years of service, Elizabeth was the GOP Senate leader's "eyes and ears on the floor." This often meant she addressed the concerns of individual Senate members about scheduling conflicts and objections to legislation before they became major issues.

Here are a couple of excerpts from *The Little Blue Book of Grieving* that Elizabeth would like to share with you:

How dependable are you to someone in your life? If you have someone in your life that you can rely on, then you are truly blessed.

If you can't think of anyone that would look to you to be that dependable one, then maybe you can start working on being that faithful and reliable person. The security you give, and the peace you receive, is born out of a loving relationship, and that loving relationship is always built on trust.

During the grieving journey, a reliable, dependable friend or family member can mean the world to someone whose life has been otherwise turned upside down due to their recent loss. This gift is easy to give and invaluable to a grieving friend or family member, so consider being someone's rock, if only for a little while.

Do you feel unsteady? The shock and unsteady feeling that you might be feeling due to the loss of your loved one is a built-in response. This is serving to cushion you when you eventually realize that you won't see your loved one again.

Even if the death is a blessing due to an illness, the shock is designed to help you process the death. Try not to fight it or work to quickly snap yourself out of it.

Elizabeth would also remind us, "If you are looking for special words to comfort someone who is grieving, look no further than within your heart. Be genuine. Be compassionate. Be sensitive. Be aware as to what not to say."

It has been my experience that it is easy to say the wrong thing without even realizing it. Individuals who recently lost a loved one are going through an extremely emotional time. In times like these, the less we say the better.

Please be careful to avoid universal clichés and statements that are likely to undermine the person's feelings or be viewed as unsympathetic. Refrain from saying things like "Time heals all wounds," "He's in a better place," "She's no longer suffering," "You'll get over it before you know it," or "Hang in there, you'll get to feeling better soon." These terms hurt instead of help.

How effective are you at comforting a victim after a death or tragedy? Do you find yourself feeling uncomfortable when you talk to someone who just experienced a tragic loss?

There are no set-in-stone rules for handling this situation, but the following may help:

- Refrain from asking about or going over the details of the event leading to the tragic situation.

- Allow an individual to go through the grieving process at a pace that individual is comfortable with. Love, not time, is the greatest healer.

- Hold back from telling the individual that you will be there when needed unless you truly mean it. And if you do, follow up continuously.

- Offer the person time to verbalize about the situation if that is what the person would like to do. Listen carefully and thoughtfully. This is not a time to offer your opinion or feelings.

- Show the person that you truly care with a statement like "You know I am here for you," or "I'm just a phone call away if you need someone to talk to."

- Reassure the individual who is continually casting blame on him- or herself that this is not the case. "You are a good person, and what happened was not punishment for something you may have done or failed to do."

- If you have been a part of the individual's life for an extended period of time, don't abruptly leave the individual with a feeling of abandonment. Stay the course.

- Appreciate that after a major loss there is no timetable for the person's returning to normal behavior. Our role is to always be an encourager regardless of the time period.

When the occasion presents itself, be ready to provide solace and comfort. But best of all, be ready to provide the encouragement to go on.

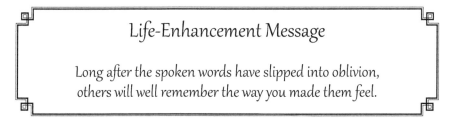

Life-Enhancement Message

Long after the spoken words have slipped into oblivion,
others will well remember the way you made them feel.

TAKING LIFE IN STRIDE

As we close this chapter, it is worth looking at some things that will help to fight emotional extremes:

- Think realistically. Learn to put things in perspective. Not getting too high or too low when confronted with a challenge can bring your stress level down.

- Manage time wisely. Controlling your time rather than having your time control you aids greatly in controlling emotions. Plan. Prepare. Perform. This is the order of events when you want to effectively limit emotional reactions.

- See problems as opportunities. Focus on solutions. When you look beyond your problems, you see a world full of opportunity.

- Be good to yourself. You cannot always count on life to treat you right, but you can make it a habit of treating yourself right.

- Laughter is therapeutic. Use humor to your advantage. Laughing is a great way to relieve tension and avoid feeling overwhelmed.

- Don't try to be a perfectionist. Strive for excellence—that will be good enough and will be a significant factor in keeping your emotions at a manageable level

- Listen attentively and carefully. Poor listening habits tend to raise the tension level because the communication process breaks down or is less effective.

- Open your mind. Opening your mind to all possibilities helps you to resist the emotion builders of negativity and pessimism.

- Prepare for key events. Preparing mentally, emotionally, and physically for important events helps you stay calm in those situations where tension is high.

- Have a physical outlet. Physical activity and exercise are a great way to deal with nervous energy and tension.

- Establish a regular routine. Exercise daily, eat balanced meals, and get adequate sleep—all are emotion reducers.

- Don't sweat the nonessential stuff, because most all of it is nonessential stuff.

- Change acceptance. Accept what you cannot change and change the things that you can. Just the thought of it takes the heat off, doesn't it?

- Do something fun. Select one fun thing to do today, and enjoy doing it with all your might.

- Improve your emotional reactions to others, for how you handle social skills is the key to influence and persuasion.

- Specify emotional areas where you need to improve to remain calm and think lucidly in stressful situations.

TWENTY-ONE

LISTEN TO YOUR HEART

There are always a lot "somebodies" out there who are going to tell you that you can't do something. But how do you know you can't do it until you attempt it for yourself?

I know from personal experience how the comments of others can weigh on the belief one has in oneself. I made a rapid rise through the St. Louis Cardinals organization, reaching the Triple A level (the highest minor league classification) by the age of twenty. There had been questions about the speed on my fastball in my previous two and a half years of pro baseball, yet I had been effective in getting batters out. That was the bottom line.

At the Triple A level, the conversations about the lack of speed on my fastball became even more pronounced. I started that season doing really well, but I began to listen to the naysayers. By season's end, I had lost my confidence. It took me two seasons before I was able to right the ship and regain my previous effectiveness. I didn't pick up any mileage on my fastball, but I became a better all-around pitcher.

As I look back, I let the wrong kind of individuals capture my ear. I was listening to those who had not been at the level that I was aspiring to. I had poisoned my strength as a baseball pitcher with doubt. I went searching for a better mousetrap when I was on the right path doing what I was doing. I learned the hard way that it is wise to take with a grain of salt the comments made by others who have never known the level that you are striving to reach.

Be careful of taking to heart the words of those who would rob you of your dreams. Their words and actions can only affect you if you allow them to. It is within your power to determine what outside forces are going to have a chance to influence you. Only one person can ultimately decide just how successful you will be. That person is you!

My advice is simple: Be your own person. Stay focused on your destination. Follow your own vision. And always listen to your heart. Your heart will let you know if what others are telling you about you is true or not.

Life-Enhancement Message

When your worth is measured by how closely you conform to the opinion of others, your worth is compromised. Your greatest strength becomes your greatest weakness. The practice of discernment is crucial in determining the people you should be listening to and those you should not listen to.

CHOOSE WISELY

Choose wisely those you listen to for advice. You stand to lose too much, associating with those who are constantly reminding you, "What makes you think you can do that?" or "There is no use in wasting your time on that." You are more apt to run into the critics when you embark on a new course or new adventure, which will often invite skepticism and doubt that will fill your text message box. Some of the comments by others, especially those close to us, can be painful to the inner being. They don't do it to be hurtful. Just the opposite. They feel like they have our best interest at heart. "I just don't want to see you make a mistake," or something along those lines, can cast doubt on your decision. The worst thing that can occur is that we let their comments leave us feeling inadequate and ill-equipped for our new venture.

Jerri Wilkins came from a family of male lawyers. She was to be the first female attorney in the family. Her father, brothers, and uncles were all elated when she graduated from law school at the top of her class.

The elder Wilkinses decided that Jerri would work for a couple of years with a firm several states away. After that tenure, she could come home and be a part of the family firm. After only six months, Jerri announced to the family that she was leaving the practice of law. She would be joining a couple of female friends to launch a corporation that would assist professional women in marketing themselves and improving their business savvy. Immediately, members of the family were at her door, questioning her wisdom. "How in the world can you do this to your family? What qualifies you to do this other job?"

A few years later, I had the pleasure of interviewing Jerri on my radio show. She and her partners had developed a sizable clientele and were looking to expand overseas. I asked Jerri, "What was behind your decision to leave the law practice?" Her response was classic: "Because I wanted to do something different. I was not excited about being a lawyer."

In the interview, Jerri had some worthy advice. She strongly suggested to "never be embarrassed by your excitement for what you are doing." She further told my audience to "think in terms of letting your excitement bring others up to your level instead of letting their lack of excitement bring you down to their level."

Jerri's story is not unique. There are plenty of them out there. You may be one of those stories. Then again, you may be a story in the making. My advice again: listen to your heart.

I have reminded young people for years: if you want to know what your future looks like, just take a look at those you associate with. The wise move is to hang out with those who

- give you a bigger concept for yourself;

- increase you, not decrease you;

- perform the way you want to perform;

- motivate you to improve and excel;

- bring out your best qualities when in their presence;

- make you think you are better than you think you are;

- do the things that you want to do, and do them well; and

- have a smile on their faces, happiness in their hearts, and optimism on their tongues.

There is little doubt that if those who share our lives don't make us better, they will eventually make us worse. Our desire to be something special is very dependent on how we handle the negative comments and interactions with those in our sphere of influence.

The message is plain enough: associate with winners. Period.

Life-Enhancement Message

Always seek the advice you need to help you perform better rather than the advice you prefer to have.

THE RIGHT KIND OF ADVICE

Let's make an about-face and seek the right kind of advice from those who can make a difference in our lives. Discernment is definitely an asset when making a determination of whom to ask for help.

The Holy Bible details how the Israelites wandered around in the desert for forty years before they were able to secure the Holy Land that God had promised them. What the male leaders obviously failed to do was seek directional assistance from the women. No doubt, the Israelites would have gotten there much sooner, don't you think?

That bit of tongue-in-cheek humor does point out a weakness that many of us have: we simply fail to ask for help when it is warranted, from someone who can offer the right kind of advice. Often, we wait until there is an emergency before we send out an SOS signal.

One of the toughest mental challenges that confront us is found in our inability to seek help when help is both needed and available. It could be something very elementary that we feel unsure or unstable about performing. Then again, it could be something that could have a dramatic effect on our future. Either way, we may lack the knowledge and expertise of some of our contemporaries who could offer some astute advice and assistance.

The most usable and persuasive wisdom comes from those who have the kind of background that we admire and respect. We tend to have faith in them because of their experience and knowledge. We are drawn to them because they have insight and an understanding of what it takes to be the kind of performer that we would like to be. They are a storehouse of good advice. We can discover gems from them that, when applied, make us better at what we do.

But you must ask. Find the common thread that runs through your job and your responsibilities, and ask questions of those whom you respect. It is amazing how accommodating others can be when you simply ask for their assistance. But once asked, you must be receptive to what they tell you.

Although there is nothing equivalent to personal experience, we are never going to live long enough to learn all on our own. "We may all possess wisdom if we are willing to be persuaded that the experience of others is as useful as our own." Sound advice from the Greek philosopher Socrates.

Why do you think people fail to ask for assistance? I think pride is a big factor. *Hey, let me show 'em what I can do* may sound good, but it has mediocrity written all over it in my book. Another reason for the failure to ask is the feeling that we don't want to impose ourselves on others. But this is a false assumption, as well. "Ask and receive" leads to the acquisition of much wisdom and know-how.

A Special Person

So many of the things that have brought us to where we are today
Are the result of someone special who helped us along the way;
Someone who believed in us when our performance was low;

Someone whose wisdom helped us choose a better way to go;
Someone who aided us in overcoming our greatest fears;
Someone whose memories made us smile across the years;
Someone who has done more than we could have ever realized;
Someone who will always be a hero in our eyes.

—Author Unknown

CAUGHT OR TAUGHT?

I really hope you believe "more is caught than is taught." Learning from the experience and expertise of others is crucial to adding value to life. The following story is a prime example of the "more is caught than taught" theme.

One of the most beautiful places I have ever visited is Monterey Bay, on the California coast. Monterey is a quaint little town nestled on the bay about seventy-five miles south of San Francisco. Before World War II most of the citizens of Monterey made their living fishing in the Pacific Ocean. Since it was a fisherman's paradise, it was also a pelican's paradise.

The pelicans did not have to fish for a living. They lived off the remains of the fish that were cleaned by the fishermen after their day's catch. Generations of the pelicans of Monterey grew up experiencing the easy life.

Then came the bombing of Pearl Harbor by the Japanese. Afterward, Japanese submarines became regular visitors along the coast, and it was rumored that an invasion of our Western shores was imminent. As a result, the fishing fleets of Monterey were grounded. With no fishing boats operating, the pelicans lost their only source of food. Only a few, if any, had ever caught a live fish. As a result, a large number of the pelicans living around Monterey Bay began to starve. It became a problem of such magnitude that the Monterey leaders decided something must be done.

Many suggestions were made, but one that became the rallying cry was, "If our pelicans don't know how to catch fish, then we must teach them how to fish."

Okay, that sounded great, but "who will teach them to fish? And how will the pelicans be taught?" Obviously, no one in Monterey had any experience teaching pelicans how to fish. The city leaders had to turn in another direction.

The answer came in the form of 150 pelicans that were captured on the Gulf Coast and shipped to Monterey. The Monterey pelicans saw the Gulf Coast pelicans swooping down and catching as many fish as they could eat. Soon the Monterey pelicans were doing the same. They learned how to fish and were saved from starvation.

There are many lessons here, but the one that stands out is the one we discussed a bit earlier: we must never lose sight of how important it is to learn from others with more know-how and experience. If we are willing to be receptive, example really is one of the greatest teachers for learning skills and techniques, methods and tactics.

Example

You want advice from those
Who have suffered and seen and know,
Who have been in the heart of the battle,
Who have given and taken many a blow,
Who never whine about their place,
Nor make excuses when things get off-track;
But stare setbacks and losses in the face,
And with determination bounce back.

You want direction from those
Who have been through thick and thin,
Who haven't strayed from the course,
Who when adversity strikes don't give in,
Who have planned and worked and given
Their very best in the midst of the fray,
Who have a strong belief in their own worth,
And know no price is too great to pay.

You want to walk with those
Who welcome the challenges they meet,
Who have a passion for prudent risk,
Who have performed many a noble feat,
Who have stared failure in the face,
Who through struggles remained strong,
Who have given their very best effort—
Yes, in their midst is where you belong.

—Adapted from an unknown source

TWENTY-TWO

HEALTH IS OUR GREATEST WEALTH

No matter what we choose to do, we are well aware that we will need to be physically and mentally fit to do it well. A guarantee at some point in life is there will be a time when past treatment of our bodies will take center stage.

Illegal drugs, alcohol, and other deterrents to good health will eventually take their toll, as will the violation of the laws of good diet, proper rest, and exercise. Sooner or later, the abuse of our bodies will leave us bankrupt of strength when strength is needed most.

The body was made to use, not abuse. When the body gives out, it takes away our positive attitude and desire to perform well. The obvious move is to minimize the use of those things that bring harm to the body and mind. Over time these things will diminish our ability to perform effectively and efficiently. When we have taken care of our bodies, we are always in a position to be physically and mentally ready for any type of action or situation.

I am a great believer that our attitudes play a crucial role in our overall health. Attitude plays a determining role in health care. It is not an exception; it is not a choice. Attitude is a necessity in maintaining quality health over the long haul.

Do you have things occurring in the near future that you look forward to with anticipation? Do you feel younger than your actual age? Do you have a strong sense of purpose? If so, you may already have taken steps to have the kind of attitude that reduces your risk of degenerative disease. And you are probably adding years to your life, as well. Study after study has shown that optimistic people have more energy, make better decisions, are more productive, are less stressed, are happier, live healthier, and live longer than their pessimistic counterparts.

Peter Nonnemann is a good example. He is the kind of person many people feel uncomfortable being around. You see, he is always upbeat and positive. His optimistic thinking has led to some very optimistic outcomes. Even around the office, Peter is a noted encourager.

He is rarely critical, focusing on how people can perform better. He makes every effort to demonstrate what it means to be a positive thinker and what it takes to maintain an optimistic mind-set.

It was on April 11, 2004, when Peter had to put his best positive thinking to work to help save his own life. He was in a terrible automobile accident on that date, one in which three people lost their lives. Every indication was that Peter wouldn't make it, either. He had many broken bones and suffered severe internal bleeding.

Peter was cognizant of his surroundings as the medics struggled to remove him from the wreckage. You would have thought that Peter was in his office as he encouraged the medics as they went about their duties. The ambulance rushed him to the hospital, and Peter was immediately hustled into the emergency room. He was still aware of his surroundings and was still being his optimistic self as the attendants prepared him for surgery.

As the doctors attended to his wounds, Peter noticed a worried look on the face of one of the nurses. He suspected that his condition was not good, and her look confirmed it. Peter's last words before he was put to sleep for life-saving surgery were, "Treat me like I'm going to live, not die." Peter lived, and he went forward with his life being his very optimistic self.

I can say this without reservation: nothing will mean more to our success than being physically and mentally ready to execute to the best of our ability every time. A positive, optimistic attitude contributes royally to making this a truism.

PAUSE FOR THE CAUSE

One of the more difficult things for assertive people to do is to take a "pause for the cause." There are times when we actually become victims of our circumstances. Events seem to rush us, press us, move us along at a pace that is injurious to our emotional and physical health. Taking a self-restoring timeout is as much about mental gain as physical gain. This timeout gives our creative juices a chance to flourish. It gives us a chance to think through ideas and solutions buried under the hustle and bustle of daily activities.

A wise move is to establish a goal-free zone where you have nothing planned; a time when there are no deadlines, responsibilities, or places to be. Such a zone allows you to unwind, regroup, and just be yourself. Although it sounds simple, the execution of a "pause for the cause" will take every ounce of mental discipline you can muster to bring about. That's because if you are not accustomed to some "me time," you are definitely going to feel uncomfortable in the beginning.

It took me to the third quarter of my life to get a handle on the importance of timeouts. I can hear someone in the back row saying, *That's because you got old.* That's probably true. I now find myself kicking back and relaxing for a few minutes every day because I'm chronologically gifted. Just for the record, I also play tennis three or four days a week. I'm blessed.

Life is to be savored. The beauty of me time is that it is precious and rare. For moments like these, you need the perfect pairing of being alone with some great relaxing music. This is my idea of quality me time. Please don't minimize the importance of a pause for the cause centered on a little me time. This is a great tool to aid in getting a new perspective on yourself and a clearer picture of where your life is headed.

> ## Life-Enhancement Message
>
> *Learn to unwind so you will have something in the
> tank when it's time to wind back up again.*

HEALTHY HABITS

Healthy habits are more than diet, working out, sleeping well, and consuming a handful of vitamins and herbals. A life filled with meaningful work, minimal stress, spiritual association, worry-free finances, solid relationship time, creative and innovative occasions for expression, and effective quiet time contributes significantly to good health.

Always be on the lookout for ways and means to develop more health-conscious habits, including the following:

- An environment free of harmful chemicals, natural disasters, and man-made hazards.

- A lifestyle that encompasses good nutrition, abundant exercise, plentiful sleep, and certainly no unhealthy addictions.

- A highly creative life that includes ample life-defining moments with others and with the environment.

- Financial stability that allows for taking care of financial obligations, present and future.

- Mental and emotional balance that allows for optimism, happiness, and satisfaction.

- Conditions that are free of oppressive and divisive factors, like fear, anxiety, and depression.

- Establishing quality relationships, including a network of family, friends, business associates, and acquaintances.

WHAT YOU EAT YOU ARE

I am a card-carrying member of the Clean Plate Club. Not that I am proud of it, but it is a statement of fat—I mean fact.

Most of us who enjoy eating experience a struggle between willpower and temptation. Willpower tends to take a back seat under these conditions: when we are stressed, experiencing boredom, feeling fatigued, or fearful. When temptation takes over we generally end up with waistlines to show it.

Dr. Ted Broer, CEO of Healthmasters.com, was a weekly contributor on my radio show. I am a big fan of Dr. Ted's because he continually emphasizes the importance of food to wellness, overall health, and longevity. Dr. Broer is a great believer that what we eat—we are.

Is it possible to train ourselves to become more conscious of our food intake? The answer is yes. I couldn't imagine cutting back on the size of the portions I ate, but, oddly enough, I did. Since my clean-plate theory went back to my childhood, I simply started eating out of a smaller plate. It worked.

Although I realize that it is no easy task to change eating habits, I am living proof that it is possible. In fact, anyone can do it if they set their mind to it. Like correcting any other longstanding habit, we must promote the aspect of mental toughness to stop overeating. A smart move is to establish a strategy for eliminating bad eating habits. Try the following on for size:

- **Set a goal.** The goal is to enjoy food more by employing a balance between what we eat and how much of it we eat. A search for balance better equips you for inhibiting overeating. It can also lead to weight loss, boosted energy, reduced cravings for junk food, and clearer thinking.

- **Stop to eat.** When it is time to eat, just eat. And sit down to do it. Drop what you are doing and focus on eating. You will enjoy it more and find that you won't need to eat as much food.

- **Sit to eat.** Eating on the run causes us to overeat later on. On the go, we are less aware of the amount of food we have consumed.

Sit down at a table to eat, even if your food is in a bag.

- **Don't shovel.** Slow down and enjoy your food. You will experience less bloating, as well. Swallowing air leads to bloating and can create gas. The same occurs when you talk with your mouth full. Take in smaller bites, eat slowly, and chew your food with your mouth closed.

- **Eat a hearty breakfast.** Studies show breakfast eaters are slimmer than those who skip breakfast. The tendency is to overeat after you have gone long periods without eating. Also, if you separate the word *breakfast* into *break-fast*, we understand even more the importance of this meal.

- **Stop eating before you are full.** Put your fork down at the first tinge of fullness. This gives your brain a chance to realize that you are full before you overdo it.

- **Eat more fruits and vegetables.** Make sure that the fruits and vegetables are natural foods. They have more nutrients than canned or packaged foods. And the less cooking of natural food, the better.

- **The meats you eat.** Eat free-range chicken, hormone-free beef, and fish like salmon, tuna, and mackerel. There are many great benefits from these meats. Fish, in particular, is loaded with essential fatty acids that are effective in the prevention of heart disease and strokes.

- **Reduce your snacks.** We tend to overindulge in calorie-laced products between meals. The best rule is to cut back on snacking. Snacking keeps the stomach "turned on," leading to the habit of overeating.

- **Watch what you snack on.** Okay. If you are a snacker, let your choice of snack fall within the 10/5/20 rule. This rule establishes that snacks should have no more 10 percent fat, 5 percent carbohydrates, and 20 percent sugar. Even then, when eating snacks, always use moderation. Make sense?

- **Eat with others.** Research shows eating with others tends to restrain our own eating behavior. We also take more time to talk and share. As a result, we eat more slowly, which registers more quickly on the brain that we are full.

- **Regular bowel movements.** Regularity and wellness depend on eating plenty of high-fiber foods, drinking plenty of water (about half of your body weight in ounces), and strenuous exercise three or four days a week. That's my personal formula.

- **Vitamins and supplements.** I strongly recommend that nutritional supplements and vitamins be taken daily. I do around fifteen daily myself, and have for over twenty years. If you take them, great. If you need to undergo a program of supplements and vitamins, do the following first:

  a) Consult with a health-care provider before taking any nutritional supplements and vitamins.

  b) Make sure nutritional supplements carry the USP label to ensure that the products meet the standards set by the US Pharmacopoeia Testing Organization.

- **Vitamin D.** A wise move is to get some vitamin D the old-fashioned way: spend no more than fifteen minutes in the midday sun without getting burned. The body stockpiles vitamin D in the liver. The absorption of calcium, which is crucial for building strong bones, is released as needed from the liver.

GET THE FOCUS RIGHT

Experts tell us that the average person makes upward of two hundred decisions a day about food and drinks. This equation points toward instituting a goal of eating only when we are hungry and stopping when we feel full. This places the accent on being more aware of our eating habits. Most diets focus on what we eat, when we should be paying more attention to why we eat and how we eat.

I certainly don't mean to minimize the importance of the foods we eat. There is little question that we should be highly aware of the harmful foods we grab on the run. I have become a big fan of organic foods and meats that are grass fed and free of growth hormones and antibiotics. This food tastes better to me, and I feel it is better for me, as well.

If we listen to what the body is telling us, we will be more cognizant of the internal cues the body gives us. When we are full, our body will let us know. When we are hungry, it provides us with feedback.

One last thing that I believe will help at the scales is focus on "crunch time." The expert opinion is to chew like a cow—slow and methodical. The crunch sound is a cue—if we listen to it—that tends to make us more aware of regulating how much food we consume.

More and more research points to the lack of proper nutrition as the cause of many of our health problems. The food we eat and the way we eat it can make a significant difference in the quality of life. It is crucial to our overall health that we be tough with ourselves at the food line. Listen to the body. It tells the whole story.

There is a touch of humor in the following messages, but also a great deal of wisdom:

- What we eat ultimately tells us what we are.

- Those who don't count calories have figures to show it.

- We think about dieting when we get thick and tired of it.

- The minutes spent at the table don't hurt us; it's the seconds.

- If you are over forty, keep an open mind and a closed refrigerator.

- Eat a breakfast for a king, a lunch for a prince, and a dinner for a pauper.

- Two of the biggest suicide weapons we can get our hands on are a knife and a fork.

- If we don't use common sense when we eat, we will end up weighing the consequences.

EXERCISE

As I mentioned earlier, three or four days a week you will find me at a tennis court. If I miss a day of tennis because of inclement weather, I will walk a couple of miles. Exercise is a vital part of my life.

Exercise is one of the essentials of a healthier life for everyone. The body was meant to be active. It actually craves physical exercise. Regular exercise is necessary for strong fitness and good health. Research shows that exercise can reduce the risk of heart disease, cancer, high blood pressure, diabetes, and other diseases. It can also improve appearance and delay the aging process. Exercise can keep us looking and feeling younger throughout our entire lives. Posture can be improved, and muscles become firmer and more toned. We not only feel better, we look better, too! You like that, don't you?

While the benefits of any exercise program are many, it is important for us to understand that exercise can have deleterious effects. Doing too much, performing intense exercises with too much regularity, and the lack of continuity can lead to muscle and tendon strains, loss of tissue, and weariness. Consistency is the key to achieving desired results.

Here are some of the other benefits of exercise that I pulled up from my database. They certainly make sense.

Exercise helps in the following ways:

- **Controls weight.** Exercise is a key to weight control because it burns calories. If we burn more calories than we take in, we lose weight, don't we? It's as simple as that.

- **Maintains mental fitness.** Physical activity engages the entire body. A healthier cardiovascular system means the heart is better able to circulate blood to all parts of the body—even to our brains, improving our mental fitness.

- **Adjusts mood.** Nothing will get us in a better mood quicker than a few minutes of exercise. Physical activity releases endorphins in the brain, creating stronger feelings of elation and satisfaction. Consistent exercise alleviates symptoms of depression, as well.

- **Strengthens the body.** Exercising with weights and other forms of resistance training builds our muscles, bones, and joints for increased strength and endurance.

- **Improves sleep.** Physical activity raises the body's core temperature, and five to six hours post-workout, the decreased core temperature signals the body to sleep. Studies show that consistent exercise results in not only less time to fall asleep, but also sounder sleep cycles, which leads to fewer daytime feelings of drowsiness.

- **Improves creativity.** An improved cardiovascular system and increased endorphins stimulate the mind for more creativity and ingenious thoughts.

- **Improves stamina.** Stamina improves as we train our bodies to become more efficient. We also use less energy for the same amount of work. The heart rate and breathing rate improve as conditioning improves. And we return to resting levels from strenuous activity sooner.

- **Enhances flexibility.** Improving our flexibility through exercise reduces the chance of injury and improves balance and coordination. If we have stiff, tense areas in the body, such as the upper back or neck, performing specific stretches can help loosen these muscles, which helps us feel more relaxed.

- **Improves appearance.** Exercise can improve appearance and delay the aging process. It can keep us looking and feeling younger. Our posture can be improved, and our muscles become firmer and toned. We not only feel better, but we look better, too!

- **Reduces stress levels.** Exercise increases the body's ability to handle stress. It is helpful in regulating areas of the brain that send stress signals. The more we train our bodies with the physical stress of exercise, the better they respond to emotional stress.

- **Other benefits.** A regular exercise program reduces the risk of a heart attack, lowers blood cholesterol levels and blood pressure, lessens the risk of type 2 diabetes and some cancers, and enhances recovery from a period of hospitalization or bed rest.

REDIRECT TO RECONNECT

Can we talk about the modern-day effects that technology has on our health? I can hear some of those who know me well hollering from the peanut gallery, *Can you believe Vickery is talking about modern technology?* Yes. And much of the stuff I am writing about here was learned the old-fashioned way. I earned it.

Most of us this day and age find our days filled with technology. Electronic devices are a part of our daily affairs. Somewhere along the line, we need to stop and ask ourselves, *Do I want to live a real life or an i-life?* Research tells us that we may not be able to do both.

Take the cell phone, for example. It is an appendage for most of us. It appears as if the phone is attached to our person. We spend hours on it, talking and texting, and we might add in a little social media, to boot.

For health reasons, is it time that we power down, disconnect, and start enjoying real life again? Research shows that high social media usage is taking a toll on healthy habits. Depression is on the rise. Anxiety levels are increasing. Stress is going through the roof. Incidents of headaches, visual fatigue, and poor-quality sleep are all surging.

Back in our discussion on monotasking, we talked about how productivity also takes a dive as a result of moving from work-related tasks to social media and back. It appears the challenge here is that the brain experiences difficulty in maintaining a train of thought. It takes several minutes for the brain to catch up when we move from a work task to a social media task, back to a work task.

How much time do you spend on the Internet? We can spend two hours with Facebook and wonder where the time went. Then there is Twitter, LinkedIn, Pinterest, Instagram, and whatever else comes down the pipe. How much value do all of these social media sites add to life?

And how about emails? Think about all the people we become accountable to through email. We spend countless time and thought power-reading and answering those emails. Now, if we mix in other work activities with answering emails, we face the same productivity problem mentioned earlier.

Over eight hours a day is now the average time a person spends on electronic instruments. That is more time than most of us spend in the bed sleeping.

It is going to take a lot of backbone to slow down this i-society that we are all wrapped up in. Do I hear you asking, *How do I power down? How do I redirect to disconnect?*

Try these ideas on for size. You might just find yourself enjoying more peace and pleasure—and yes, better health!

- Place your cell phone facedown when you are sharing time with friends or enjoying a meal with family.

- Eliminate receiving emails via your phone. Checking your laptop or PC a couple of times a day will suffice, won't it?

- Take a twenty-four-hour break. Give all your electronic devices a twenty-four-hour break over the weekend. You will not have a heart attack, but you might prevent one.

- Charge your cell phone in your bathroom, not your bedroom. Use an old-time alarm clock if you need a wake-up call. Keep the temptation of the phone hidden away.

- What are all the electronic diversions taking you away from? Maybe a better question is, What are you missing by spending a big part of your spare time on social media? How about a real, live conversation or a nice, brisk walk?

- Out on a dinner date? Leave your phone in the car. *What if I get an emergency call?* How many of those have you received in your lifetime? Lighten up and enjoy yourself.

- Use the thirty-minute rule: refuse to use all technology the first thirty minutes and the last thirty minutes of the day. This just might contribute to greater peace of mind.

- You have a legitimate right to unplug your devices and redirect your connections to real, live people. Try it. You might like it.

Living and functioning in the i-world is a reality. But let's not do it at the expense of our health. It is possible to have balance. What we lose in the world of devices, we can gain in the world of health.

A FINAL NOTE

You are at the end, headed toward a new beginning. I am delighted you have made it this far. But here you are, a new you. You have discovered more of who you are and what you are. You are ready to reach beyond and tackle your world on your own terms.

You have a great game plan in hand. That game plan includes a newfound awareness of the necessary order of things going forward. You are now prepared to reach out and grab hold of possibilities that reach beyond what you have experienced in the past. Now, when you look at that mountain in front of you, you will be able to see a light at the end of an unbuilt tunnel.

Now there is only one thing left for you to do: execute. You are properly equipped to implement and perform. The key factor in this mission is consistency. Real transformation doesn't happen without consistency. Striving for consistency in your daily activity pattern and behavior is not a some-of-the-time thing, it is an all-of-the-time thing. Consistency keeps you in sync with progression.

There will be times when the old ways will beckon you to return. You have gotten this far, so there is no turning back now. Stay the course and you will emerge on the other side a wiser and stronger person. That's good stuff. That's what I am wishing for you.

ACKNOWLEDGMENTS

My staff and I have done enormous research to locate the original writers and provide proper credit for portions of the material used in the book. If corrections or credit is needed, we will make the adjustment in future printings.

There are a great number of people I am deeply indebted to. I am thankful and grateful to Tim Neller for his great editing work and the time he spent on the final manuscript.

Dr. David Dyson, who spent many hours with me on the manuscript, is another person who played a key role in this project becoming a reality. A very special thanks also goes to Debra Watson, who was a whiz at content editing. She added immensely to many of the chapters in the book. And a debt of gratitude goes to Dana Vickery, who was a solid sounding board on many topics in the book.

Janet Perez Eckles, Steve McMillian, Bob Beauprez, Elizabeth Chryst, and Jason Will all stroked the editing pen across many pages. There were others who contributed time and talent to this project who prefer to go unnamed.

ABOUT THE AUTHOR

Lou Vickery has had four different professional careers: professional baseball player (ten years), stockbroker (four years), sales-and-marketing trainer (twenty-nine years), and radio talk show host (fourteen years). This broad and varied background offers Lou an excellent platform for sharing what it takes to be successful in today's world.

Lou earned his BS degree from Troy State University College of Education during 1959–68, mostly in the offseason from his baseball career. Lou was with both the St. Louis Cardinals and the New York Yankees organizations during his professional baseball career.

Reach Beyond is Lou's fourteenth published book, with two more in the works. His most recent release was *Motor-vators: For Salespeople Destined for Greatness.* Other books by Lou that are still in print include *A Touch of Gray* (his first novel), *The Rise of the Poarch Band of Creek Indians*, *Good Stuff for the Journey*, and *Forty Love* (for tennis players). These can be found at Amazon or at www.louvickerybooks.com.

Lou resides in Fairhope, Alabama, where he spends his time writing, assisting his ninety-six-year-old mother, and playing tennis three or four days a week.

CPSIA information can be obtained
at www.ICGtesting.com
Printed in the USA
LVHW082319021020
667790LV00014B/1875

9 781950 906635